In her book, Marilyn Heavilin speaks
not only from experience, but from a rich
as powerful as her message is, Marilyn
that draws the reader in. Whether you nee
you'll be helped greatly by *Roses in December.*

Joni Eareckson Tada

This is a much needed book, especially in a day when success and
happiness are being equated with Christian fidelity. Many suffer who are
very faithful to God. This is both scriptural and experiential. Thousands
of grieving, hurting, and helping people will profit from this book.

Jay Kesler, President
Taylor University

This book is a rare treasure! It is based on the multiple loss experiences
of a woman and her family who dealt with grief in a healthy manner,
combined with her experiences in reaching out to others who also experienced loss. As a professional, I was greatly aided by reading such a clear
presentation of the grieving process as it occurred over a period of years,
giving me invaluable insights and a basis for practical application. I strongly
recommend this book to other therapists who value a lucid, first-hand
presentation of the experience of loss and healthy working-through.

William G. Britt III, Ph.D.
Clinical Psychologist
Assistant Professor of Psychiatry
Loma Linda University Medical School

This book provides three critically essential assurances for the grieving:
That others have hurt like they do, that there is hope and healing for the
agony of grief and loss, and that, through Christ, not only acceptance but
victory is possible. Those who hurt the most should read it first.

Larry W. Poland, Ph. D.
Director of Ministries
Trinity Evangelical Free Church

From heartache to healing — an intimate chronicle of a journey through
grief. It is possible to identify significant steps in the process of healing.
This book offers hope to those in their own private pain of loss.

Carol Ann Frizzell, R.N.
Hospice Coordinator
Redlands Community Hospice

Roses in December contains penetrating insights into how to deal with
grief personally and practical suggestions for others who desire to give
help that is helpful. I learned that recovery from tragedy cannot be rushed.
Pushing or pulling to try and speed up the process fails miserably. This
book encourages all of us to give careful consideration to what we say
and do before it is said and done and will be helpful for people of all ages.

Ted Ewing, Youth Pastor

Roses in December is a phenomenal book. I have ordered two full cases
for my personal use and I plan to send them to friends who are experiencing
loss. I thank God that Marilyn is willing to share this marvelous testimony
of how God helped her family when they were hurting.

Dr. Bill Bright, President
Campus Crusade for Christ

To Jimmy, Nathan, and Ethan
Three beautiful flowers
in my bouquet of
December Roses

To Glen,
Matt and Debbie,
Mellyn and Mike
Your love and encouragement
have kept me going.

Roses
in
December

MARILYN WILLETT HEAVILIN

Here's Life Publishers

Published by
Here's Life Publishers
P.O. Box 1576
San Bernardino, California 92402

HLP Product Number 951699
© 1986, Marilyn Willett Heavilin
All rights reserved.
Printed in the United States of America.

Library of Congress Cataloging-in-Publication Data

Heavilin, Marilyn Willett.
   Roses in December.

   1. Consolation.   2. Suffering — Religious aspects —
Christianity.   3. Heavilin, Marilyn Willett.
4. Christian biography — United States.   I. Title.
BV4905.2.H42   1987   248.8'6   86-22861
ISBN 0-89840-165-8

Author Photo Courtesy of C.R. Noon

Unless otherwise indicated, Scripture references are from the King James Version of the Bible. Scriptures indicated TLB are from The Living Bible, © 1971 by Tyndale House Publishers, Wheaton, Illinois.

FOR MORE INFORMATION, WRITE:
L.I.F.E. — P.O. Box A399, Sydney South 2000, Australia
Campus Crusade for Christ of Canada — Box 300, Vancouver, B.C. V6C 2X3, Canada
Campus Crusade for Christ — Pearl Assurance House, 4 Temple Row, Birmingham B2 5HG, England
Lay Institute for Evangelism — P.O. Box 8786, Auckland 3, New Zealand
Great Commission Movement of Nigeria — P.O. Box 500, Jos, Plateau State Nigeria, West Africa
Campus Crusade for Christ — P.O. Box 240, Colombo Court Post Office, Singapore 9117
Campus Crusade for Christ International — Arrowhead Springs, San Bernardino, CA 92414, U.S.A.

FIRST PRINTING, FEBRUARY 1987
SECOND PRINTING, JUNE 1987
THIRD PRINTING, SEPTEMBER 1987
FOURTH PRINTING, MAY 1988

Contents

October 2, 1982 — Getting
ready for a cross-country race

February 15, 1983

Foreword

It was twenty years ago I first met Marilyn Heavilin when we were both new staff members for Campus Crusade for Christ. We soon found we had many things in common including the loss of two boy babies apiece.

We both loved teaching Bible studies and we joined our efforts in teaching a group of sixty to eighty women weekly in my home. Our friendship has continued through the years and as Marilyn attended Christian Leaders and Speakers Seminars (CLASS) and became excited about sharing her experiences with others, I had the joy of encouraging and training her to become the outstanding speaker she is today.

Her message in *Roses in December* is so beautifully composed that it is almost poetic and Marilyn has managed to write positively on a subject which could be negative, and to give the Lord glory when she could have opted for a saga of self-pity.

Marilyn has generously given her time to uplift those who are hurting and when I find bereaved parents in my travels and give them Marilyn's card, she is always willing to counsel them on the phone and show them the path to inner peace in difficult or traumatic situations.

I read this manuscript in its beginning stages and again at completion and I heartily recommend this to

all women, counselors, pastors, parents, and especially
teens and young adults. Everyone needs to read *Roses
in December.*

Florence Littauer
Founder and President
Christian Leaders and
        Speakers Seminars (CLASS)

The Rose
of
Preparation

Even when walking through the dark valley of death I will not be afraid, for you are close beside me, guarding, guiding all the way (Psalm 23:4, TLB).

I sat across the table from my friend Mary, silently sipping tea, waiting for her to speak. Her son had died just two weeks before. She started to speak several times, but her words were choked back by her sobs. Finally she took a deep breath and blurted out, "No one understands my grief. I feel so alone."

If you have recently experienced a heartbreak, perhaps you are also acquainted with the feelings of isolation and loneliness. It is true that no one else can understand your grief completely or feel your individual pain, but I have experienced loss. I've lived through my own grief: the disappointments, the shattered dreams, the fears, the depression, and the emotional pain that made my whole body ache. I remember feeling, too, that no one else could possibly understand, but I've discovered it is possible to walk through that long, cold winter season of grief and emerge on the other side a whole, healthy person.

Dear friend, you don't have to go through your grief alone. Please let me join you in this winter season and share my very special December roses with you. The first rose along our path is the rose of preparation.

It was a cold, blustery February evening when my mom and I climbed aboard the Greyhound bus and I excitedly waved goodbye to my daddy. We were going to a small town in northern Michigan to visit my grandparents, my aunt and uncle, and best of all, my four-month-old cousin, Mary Beth. Now she would be old enough to respond to me. I could hardly wait. I'd been praying for a baby brother or sister as long as I could remember, but since my prayer hadn't been answered, I doted on cousin Mary Beth.

As soon as Grandpa lifted me from the bus steps, I asked, "When can we see Mary Beth?" and was very disappointed when he said I'd have to wait until morning. I climbed in bed with Grandpa and Grandma before dawn and asked, "Can we go now?"

As I gobbled down my breakfast, I saw my aunt and uncle's truck coming up the lane. I anxiously met them at the door, but this unsuspecting, innocent four-year-old knew something was wrong when I saw the pain on their faces. Mary Beth wasn't with them.

We all stood in that old farm kitchen with the snow piled high against the stone walls and windows, and my Uncle Louie began to explain. He told us that Mary Beth had suffocated in the night. She was dead.

I can still hear my own screams as I ran across the lane to my great-grandmother's home next door. "My baby's dead! My baby's dead!"

My screaming must have torn at the breaking hearts of the adults, but no one reproved me. They just picked me up and hugged me as we cried together.

The snowstorm had closed the roads from town to my aunt's house, and when Uncle Louie had called the coroner and undertaker, he found out that they would have to wait for the snowplow — it could be hours before they arrived.

Our family all drove to my aunt and uncle's cottage where a kind neighbor waited with Mary Beth's still form.

I insisted on seeing "my baby," and no one had the strength to resist me. She had been a beautiful baby, but the black and blue blotches that come with suffocation had stolen her beauty. I didn't care — she was still my Mary Beth. I sat by the bed, stroked her hand, and talked to her. She felt like a china doll — cold and unresponsive.

In those wintry hours my family was able to deal with their grief and to say goodbye privately to our sweet little Mary Beth. My fear of death waned as my mom explained that Jesus was taking care of Mary Beth and someday I would see her again. My fear of dead bodies lessened as I touched Mary Beth and realized she wasn't in that body anymore.

That was my first but not my last contact with death as a child. By the time I was twelve, my paternal grandparents, my great-grandmother, a thirteen-year-old cousin, and a seventeen-year-old cousin had died. Even my Aunt Lucille and Uncle Louie died after their gas stove exploded and caused a flash fire. It was through that tragedy that I got my long-awaited little brother Walt — my parents adopted the youngest of Aunt Lucille and Uncle Louie's three orphaned children.

Death was no stranger to my family, but I don't look back to a childhood filled with tragedy and sad memories. I remember a family made strong through sorrow, a family with a tenacity that triumphed over troubles, and a family that cried and laughed together.

After my husband Glen and I were married, we had three children, Matthew, Mellyn (our only girl), and Jimmy. Our life seemed ideal. Glen was an executive with General Motors, we had a new home, and we were on our way to a successful life.

Early one morning Glen went in to make a routine check on the children, but suddenly his voice penetrated my slumber, "Marilyn, call the doctor — Jimmy's gone."

With my heart pounding and my mind racing, I obediently called our personal friend and physician. "Tom, come quick, it's Jimmy!" But I knew Glen must be mistaken.

I quickly hung up the phone and raced into Jimmy's room in time to see Glen trying to breathe life into our young son. As my eyes fixed on Jimmy's lifeless form with black and blue blotches, I gasped, "Mary Beth!" The memories came tumbling back in a wave. Could this be happening again?

While waiting for the doctor, Glen and I knelt, with the baby still in his arms, and we prayed, "Jesus, please use this situation for Your honor and glory."

The autopsy said "interstitial pneumonia." Today we would probably classify this as a crib death.

Jimmy died more than twenty-two years ago, but as I write this account some scenes are still very vivid: the hurt I heard in my mother's voice as we called with the terrible news; the panic I felt later that day when the thought crossed my mind, *I haven't fed Jimmy!* and then the wave of grief as I realized Jimmy was dead; the feeling of rage mixed with overwhelming sadness that I experienced when I went into Jimmy's room and discovered that well-meaning friends had removed all of Jimmy's furniture and clothing without my knowledge or permission. I also recall dreading to meet people on the street or in the grocery store because I didn't want to answer the question, "How's your baby doing?"

Glen and I trusted the Lord and were able to go on with our lives, though it was hard when we were told, "You can still have lots of babies, and you'll probably forget all about this."

A year and a half later we were delighted with the doctor's announcement that we were going to have twins. I reasoned that God was "paying us back" for the child He had taken. It's amazing how we try to fit God into our mindset.

Our identical twin boys, Nathan James and Ethan Thomas, were born on Christmas morning, 1965. What a celebration we had! I received dozens of phone calls and bouquets. We were sure the birth of twins would lessen the pain of Jimmy's death.

We took Nathan home on New Year's Eve, but Ethan needed to gain a little weight. Each day I checked on Ethan and his progress was good. But on the ninth day his weight began going down and he was lethargic. Specialists were called in: diagnosis — pneumonia; prognosis — not good.

I was angry at life and at God. What had we done to deserve this? We were strong Christians, actively serving the Lord, and we had accepted Jimmy's death without bitterness or anger. Was this our thanks?

I struggled with God all night, and the next morning as I read out of *Streams in the Desert,* I thought I had found my answer. The verse for that day was "Go thy way; thy son liveth" (John 4:50).

I called all of my friends. "I'm sure Ethan will be fine. I'm sure that's what this verse means." Once again I thought I had God all figured out, but that evening as I pressed my face against the nursery window and watched my dear little Ethan labor with each breath, God spoke to me very clearly. "Marilyn, I loved you enough to *die* for you; aren't you willing to trust Me with this child?"

In an attempt to get alone with God, I went into the bathroom in the private room the hospital had given us, locked the door, slumped to the floor, and cried out to God. "This isn't fair. We're good people, good parents, good Christians. Why should this happen to us?"

Once I had blurted out my feelings, I sat silently for a while and then a peace began to grow within me. My prayer continued, "Lord I don't understand this, and I certainly don't like it. But I love You and I trust You. I give You complete control over Ethan's life. Now You must give me the strength to live through this." A few minutes later Ethan joined his brother Jimmy in heaven.

I leaned my head heavily against Glen's shoulder as we drove silently home. The snow glistened in the moonlight and I could hear the crunch of our tires against the frozen slush on the highway. My mind drifted back to that verse, "Go thy way; thy son liveth." What did it mean to me now?

Glen and I were in the process of joining a Christian organization in California. We were leaving our home, our family, and our friends. I *sensed* God was saying through that verse, "Marilyn, continue with your plans; serve Me with all your heart; and don't worry about Ethan or Jimmy. They're both living with Me, and they're fine." I now believe that was what God was saying, but I couldn't *receive* that interpretation until I had yielded *my* will to His.

I experienced many of the same adjustments after Ethan died as I had after Jimmy's death. We already had sent out birth announcements and an article had appeared in our local paper, so during the first few weeks after Ethan died, we often received congratulation cards and sympathy cards in the same mail. I recall receiving two beautiful baby blue suits accompanied with a note, "Twins! I think you're one of the luckiest couples in the world!"

I didn't feel lucky; I felt plagued because our troubles were continuing. Shortly after Jimmy died I had begun to have a problem with recurring ovarian cysts which required several surgeries. Five weeks after Ethan died, the pain began again. I had another cyst. We consulted several doctors who all recommended that I have a total hysterectomy. After losing two babies in less than two years, the hope for more children was gone. While some of my friends were crying because of too many pregnancies, I was crying because I would never be pregnant again.

A month after that surgery, my grandmother died. As the family was preparing to leave the house for Grandma's funeral, Glen developed a migraine headache and went to bed. Then I began sobbing so violently someone had to give me a tranquilizer to calm me down enough that I could attend the funeral. People couldn't understand why Glen and I were having such a difficult time with my grandmother's death. After all, she was in her seventies, she had lived a good life, and she didn't suffer long. None of us took time to consider what Glen and I had been through in the past year and a half. And the following year we moved four times, including one move from Indiana to California.

We had moved from a large home into a tiny, two-bedroom apartment with rented furniture, and Matt and Mellyn were to sleep in bunk beds with Nate's crib in the same tiny room. The very first evening Glen had to work late so I began trying to get Matt and Mellyn settled into bed by myself. Just as they climbed in, the top bunk came crashing down on top of Mellyn!

Except for a few bumps and bruises, she was not injured, but the children all became hysterical. Overwhelmed and crying myself, I collapsed in the middle of the floor, and tried to comfort my three screaming children, all the while thinking, *And this is the great adventure God has called me to?*

When Nate was about eight months old, I went into a severe depression. I couldn't sleep; I cried a lot; and when I wasn't crying I was yelling at the children.

Glen was very patient with me but he didn't know what was wrong. My Christian friends were certain it was a spiritual problem, and they kept asking, "Are you sure you understand the Spirit-filled life?"

My mother came to visit, took one look at me, and said, "This girl needs to go to bed." I had been running and running from my pain, but it finally had caught up with me.

No one had warned me that it was necessary to grieve, nor did anyone explain that, even though I had a baby and two other children to take care of, I would still miss Jimmy and Ethan. I was told that the adjustment to a hysterectomy was all in my head, and I was not informed about the changes that would occur in my body. Three babies, two funerals, four surgeries, and four moves in twenty-four months and I was only twenty-seven. No wonder I was depressed!

My mother gave me the physical help I needed, the children matured, and I slowly grew accustomed to my grief. As the years went by I spent my time with my family, and God allowed the empty spots in my heart to be filled to some extent by other children, especially boys, who needed the attention I had time to give. We cooked for the band and bolstered the high school football team. Matt and Mellyn participated in various activities, and Glen, Nate, and I became their cheering section. Matt and Mellyn graduated and went on to college. In 1982, Mellyn married Mike Savage, a young man I had led to the Lord earlier.

That fall Nate began his junior year in high school. He had grown into a tall, handsome, sixteen-year-old young man. He was on the cross-country and basketball teams, sang in the ensemble, played trumpet in the pep band, and was on the honor roll.

Since I worked at the Christian high school where he attended, Nate and I spent a lot of time together driving to and from school. Although he was a very quiet boy, occasionally he shared something that gave me a hint of what was going on in his mind.

One morning as we were driving to school, he said, "Mom, have you ever wondered what Ethan looks like?"

I said, "Well, honey, you were identical twins; he must look just like you."

There was quiet for a moment, and then Nate said wistfully, "Boy, I sure would like to see him."

I chuckled rather uneasily trying to cover up the strange feeling that flooded over me and replied, "Well, when we get to heaven, we'll all get to see him, and Jimmy, too."

The Rose
of
Sorrow

And now, dear brothers, I want you to know what hap-
pens to a Christian when he dies so that when it happens,
you will not be full of sorrow, as those are who have no
hope (I Thessalonians 4:13, TLB).

O n February 10, 1983, as we arrived at school,
Nate scurried off with his friends to leave for
a field trip. The day before I had heard him
ask his brother Matt, "Hey brother, how would you
like to take a day off work?" Nate explained that his
class was going to Los Angeles and they needed more
cars and drivers. I wasn't surprised when Matt agreed
to drive. He always was a softy when it came to his
little brother.

Nate hardly had time to talk with me between his
return from the field trip and leaving for the evening's

basketball game. In fact, he was trotting backwards down the hall when I asked him what time he would be home.

"Oh, I don't know. The game might run kinda late, and it will take a while for the drive home. I'll call you if we're going to be really late."

He gave a quick wave, and called, "See ya later, Mom," as he dashed to his locker to get his uniform and gym bag.

That night my husband Glen went to his college class, and I spent a quiet evening alone. My mom called from San Diego where she and Dad were camping with some friends, and Mellyn called to check on details of the homecoming game the next evening at Nate's school. As I tried to watch television, I kept falling asleep, so I finally went to bed and slept soundly.

Suddenly, I awoke.

Where was I?

Why wasn't Glen in bed with me?

My thoughts were all jumbled. What time was it? My sleep-blurred eyes eventually focused on the clock. 11:44. I hurried down the hall to find Glen.

"Isn't Nate home yet?"

Glen shook his head.

With much uneasiness, I said, "Something must be wrong. He always calls if he's going to be late."

I tried to appear calm for Glen, but on the inside, I was crying, *Please bring him home, Lord; please bring him home.*

At first we hesitated to call anyone. "Surely it is just car trouble. He'll call us soon," we reasoned. This was a new experience for us. Nate was always good about calling. My pride made it difficult for me to call others and admit I didn't know where my son was. But as it grew later and later, alarm overruled pride.

After several calls to Nate's coaches, we tried calling

a friend who always rode with Nate. The sick feeling
in my stomach grew when there was no answer at his
house.

I thought, *His family never stays out late; they must
have heard something. Why haven't we?*

Glen called another of Nate's friends, but her mom
answered. Soon I heard Glen say, "What hospital are
they in?"

As Glen was dialing the hospital, he said, "There's
been a terrible head-on collision. All of the kids who
were in Nate's car are in the hospital." The emergency
room attendant told Glen they had a young male,
listed as John Doe. I heard Glen say, "Does that mean
he's dead?"

"He's alive but he's unconscious and unable to identify himself." The attendant continued, "Mr. Heavilin,
come quickly."

I knocked on Matt's bedroom door, "Honey, there's
been a bad accident. Get dressed quickly; we must
hurry!"

Matt recalls:

> Mom didn't say who was in the accident.
> Grandma and Grandpa Willett were out of
> town that night — it could have been them.
> But I knew it was Nate. As I was numbly
> getting dressed, I thought, "We're going
> through another funeral."

At twenty-four Matt was already well acquainted
with grief.

It seemed I was moving in slow motion. I desperately
needed to get to Nate and kept telling myself everything
would be all right once we got there. I knew if I could
touch him and speak to him, he would wake up. In
my mind, I was talking to Nate all the while I was

dressing. *Hang on, Nate. I'm coming; I'm coming. Just hang on.*

Our minds were in a fog, but we were functioning automatically in an organized manner. Matt remembered to take rolls of coins for phone calls, and I grabbed my address book, thinking, *We've got to call everybody and tell them to pray.* Then I thought of Glen's and my parents. How could we tell them Nate might be dying? Grandchildren aren't supposed to die.

It was the middle of the night and everything seemed so still. We passed the parents of one of the girls who'd been in Nate's car, heading to another hospital. We rolled down the car windows to exchange information.

"How's your daughter?" we asked.

"She's conscious and has many facial injuries. How's Nate?"

"He's unconscious — listed as a John Doe. Pray!"

As Glen drove, I prayed. The first of my prayer was simply, "God, is it happening again? We've already lost two children. Do we have to bear that pain again?"

At the hospital we hurried to the reception desk, "Where's Nate? How is he? Can we see him?" So many questions and no answers.

The nurse just said, "Someone will be out to see you shortly; please fill out these forms."

We struggled to focus our minds on car license numbers and insurance information. Finally Glen talked with a police officer who verified the car involved in the crash was ours, but told us nothing about Nate. He said the accident occurred at 11:44, the exact time I had awakened so suddenly! How thankful I am God awakened me so we were able to get to the hospital before it was too late.

A security guard appeared, saying, "Clear the halls. We're bringing a patient through." We stood in a doorway to watch.

Several people huddled over the person on the cart, but I could see a head of tousled brown hair, a pair of blue jeans, and a big foot wearing a white sock. Just as the cart was pushed out of sight, I realized it was Nate. I wanted to run after him, but instead I just stood there numbly, trying to take in what I had seen.

My son, my Nate, lying on that cart, so helpless; my son who had looked anything but helpless as he grabbed his uniform and left for a physically taxing evening of basketball. "Oh God, please help him; please help us," I whispered.

Soon a nurse called us into a small, cluttered office, and in a warm, but very concerned voice, she said, "We have just taken your son to surgery. His leg has been crushed; he has brain damage and extensive damage to his heart and lungs. His heart stopped once already, and we opened his chest to massage the heart and start it again."

I felt sick as I envisioned someone's hands on my son's heart. My thoughts drifted back to the prayer I had prayed on the way to the hospital.

Lord, please don't let it be Nate's fault. Please heal all of the kids if it's Your will. Lord . . . I hesitated and began again, *Lord, we want Your will in Nate's life, and Lord, we're giving You power of attorney over Nate.*

As the nurse continued, I began to sense what God's will was for Nate. I asked the nurse, "Do you think he's going to make it?"

Her eyes dropped, and she shook her head, "No."

A kind-looking woman came up to me and said, "My brother was the driver of the other car. I'm so sorry. I'm so sorry. Is your son going to be all right?"

I answered very matter-of-factly, "My son is dying."

As she began to weep, I instinctively wrapped my arms around her ample frame and said, "It's OK. If Nate dies, I know he'll go to heaven and I'll see him again someday."

The lady stiffened a little and walked away. Perhaps my comments seemed too unfeeling, too calloused. They weren't meant to be. I realize now I was in the numbness of grief. God was speaking for me.

As Mellyn and Mike arrived, we hugged each other tightly, prayed, and waited. Eventually we learned that the three other students in Nate's car were seriously injured, but the doctors said they would survive. A prayer answered.

We also had learned the man who hit Nate had been arrested for drunk driving. I experienced anger and relief at the same time. It wasn't Nate's fault, another prayer answered, but my son was dying because someone had been foolish enough to drink and drive. My son, who never drank and who was from a family who didn't drink, was the victim of a drunk driver. How unfair!

The words "drunk driver" were still spinning in my mind as the nurse re-entered the waiting room. When I saw her face, I knew.

"Is he gone?"

She nodded, "Yes."

Glen came from around the corner, and I said, "Honey, he's gone." The hope left his eyes as he hugged me tightly and we wept.

Four years have passed since that agonizing evening, years filled with a melange of emotions and questions. Why *our* son? Why did he have to die? Will the sick feeling in my stomach ever go away? Why didn't we at least have time to say goodbye?

I have felt *anger* at a justice system that doesn't protect us from such happenings; *jealousy* toward others whose lives seem to go untouched; *resentment* that it was my son instead of someone else's.

However, as I walked into Nate's memorial service and saw nearly a thousand people in attendance, I realized that God had allowed Nate to touch more lives in seventeen years than many of us touch in seventy; many of them young lives, people who still can have years of service for God.

Even now as I reread the numerous newspaper articles, including one with the headline: "Nathan lives now in his heavenly, not Heavilin home," I feel confident that Nate was a witness to the entire community for his Lord Jesus, especially in his death.

His death also caused some adults to change their priorities. After Nate died, a co-worker of Glen's began attending his own son's track meets regularly — time with his son has become very precious.

A few weeks later a college representative was in my office and I shared my story with her. She asked, "Considering what you've just been through, do you have any specific advice for other parents?"

I responded, "Spend all of the time you can with your family. Always keep them on the top of your priority list." The next day she wrote me a letter.

"I want you to know that as a result of my conversation with you on Wednesday, I've canceled all my appointments for today and I'm going home to my son — first to attend his baseball game, then home to be with him."

I quickly saw God allow us to influence lives around us because of our experience.

One month after Nathan's death, some of my students and I visited Biola University. As we rested in our dorm room we talked about what it was going to be like living without Nate. They commented:

"It's no fun at school anymore."

"I don't like to watch the basketball games now."

"There's no one to sing in the halls with me."

Then someone asked, "How can we ever enjoy Christmas again since Nate's birthday is Christmas Day?"

I muttered, "I'd like to ask God to cancel December because I don't want any part of Christmas." The thought of gifts, Christmas carols, and Christmas programs seemed incongruous with what we were facing.

The next morning the students visited classes, and my friend Diana and I wandered around the campus, ending up at the bookstore. I was aimlessly leafing through the display of posters when one caught my eye. I couldn't believe it. Through my tears, I called to Diana, "Come and look at this!"

The poster was a beautiful red rose. The flower had opened and dewdrops were visible on the petals. At the bottom was a quote which conveyed a message from God to me that day.

It read, "GOD GIVES US MEMORIES SO WE MIGHT HAVE ROSES IN DECEMBER."[1]

My first thought was, *God, you've got to be kidding. Even in California we don't find many roses in December, and there certainly aren't any roses in my life right now.*

But I bought the poster, had it framed, and hung it in my bedroom. I glanced at it frequently and seemed to hear God say, "Marilyn, I'm not going to cancel December, but I've given you many, many wonderful memories of Nate. Gather and savor them because through those memories and through the special things I'm going to do for you this year and every year, you're going to have bouquets of roses, even in December. Keep looking for the roses!"

God is continually keeping His promise by providing roses, sometimes with actual flowers, sometimes through friends, and often in the form of memories as a reminder He is caring for me, and when I hurt, He hurts.

A few months later I was helping a student with a scholarship notebook she had compiled. It included certificates showing her accomplishments, and pictures from high school yearbooks. I turned to a page with a group picture, and I didn't see anything else, only that Nate was in the picture. When I saw it, I was overwhelmed with sorrow and began to cry.

At that moment, Sally, the school secretary came into my office unaware of what had just happened. She was holding a rose.

She explained, "I bought this rose for someone else, but she isn't here today, and God just told me I should bring it to you!"

In the years since Nate's death, hardly a moment has gone by without me thinking of him. Knowing that God cares doesn't take the hurt away, but it does make the hurt bearable.

We have gathered many memories, each a beautiful rose.

One of my young friends, Darcy, gave me a notepad which states, "A rose is God's autograph." As I stroll in my rose garden of memories, I see God's autograph everywhere. Each rose is a special, signed gift from God reminding me of His care. And when the hurts become more than I can bear, it seems He always sends me another rose — a beautiful memory or a precious friend.

God continues to increase my bouquet of roses. Some have come with thorns, but God has helped me deal even with the thorns.

Perhaps you are going through a December in your life; a death, a divorce, or some other severe disappointment, and you can't see any roses. Let me share my December roses with you so you can start collecting a bouquet of your own and then share your roses with others.

The Rose of Comfort

Rejoice with them that do rejoice, and weep with them that weep (Romans 12:15).

W hen we left the hospital after Nathan's death, the many friends who were waiting for us wanted to know, "What can we do for you?"

My response was, "Come home with us," because we did not want to walk into our house alone. We arrived at our home after 3 A.M., and within an hour, more than forty people were with us sitting in our living room having a prayer meeting.

Their friendship, even in the middle of the night, comforted me immeasurably. As we prayed, I sensed we were not the only ones who were grieving — we were not the only ones who would miss Nathan.

I will always remember my friend Donna Lynn's prayer because she thanked God for the memories and asked Him to help us concentrate on the good times. Her prayer came from the heart of one mother and touched the heart of another. At that moment, all I could remember were the times I had been upset with Nate and had made wrong decisions, but Donna Lynn's prayer helped me focus on the good times. I began to see that even though there were a few times I would like to have changed, the good memories far outweighed the not-so-good ones. Her positive prayer was an encouragement and a comfort.

Early that morning, Vonette Bright arrived. After speaking at a prayer breakfast where she had shared about our tragedy, she came directly to our home.

Following her message, a young couple had come to her and said, "Vonette, we have a verse we would like you to take to your friend." When Vonette arrived at our home, she was excited even though she was broken for us. The verse reads:

> The good men perish; the godly die before their time. . . . No one seems to realize that God is taking them away from evil days ahead. For the godly who die shall rest in peace (Isaiah 57:1,2, TLB).

Five people shared the same verse with us by noon that day. Later I discovered that J. Vernon McGee had preached on the same passage that morning on the radio. What timing!

Through it, God said to me, "Marilyn, it wasn't an accident. I wasn't on vacation the night Nate died. I knew about it before it happened. Marilyn, I'm taking him away from something worse. He's with Me, and he's doing fine."

Over the years I've observed that, for the Christian, there are many things worse than death. I may not know until eternity all that God spared Nathan, but I can rest assured from now until then that Nate is with the Lord, and he is doing fine. I am so thankful Vonette took the time to visit me. My whole outlook might have been different if I hadn't received her comforting words.

However, not all the words we received were comforting. Have you ever, in your eagerness to be helpful, said something that you realized afterward could cause problems? Something like that was said to me. While we were waiting at the hospital, I received a phone call from an acquaintance asking how Nate was doing. By then God had confirmed in my heart that Nate wasn't going to live, so I simply said, "Nate is dying." I expected her response to be similar to ours, feeling hurt, crushed, and disappointed.

Her response was different. She exclaimed, "Oh no, you can't give up. Death comes from Satan. If you give up, you're giving in to Satan, and if Nate dies, it will be because you gave up."

As I hung up the phone, I saw the nurse coming to tell us Nate was dead. The words rang in my ears, "Nate died because you gave up."

As we walked out of the hospital into the parking lot, I asked God to give me a verse which would comfort me. Part of one verse, "Precious in the sight of the Lord is the death of His saints" (Psalm 116:15), and the principle taught in another, "Even before we are formed, our days are numbered" (Psalm 139:16), came to me immediately.

Later, however, the woman's words came back to haunt me again and again. Glen helped me resolve the matter when he said, "Marilyn, you never gave up on Nate, but you gave OVER to God."

Glen was right. He reminded me of the prayer I had prayed on the way to the hospital. "God, we give You power of attorney in Nathan's life. We trust he is going to be fine, but if that isn't Your will, it's OK. We are turning the controls over to You."

Whenever I saw this lady after Nate's death, I had to remind myself, "I didn't give up; I gave over." In my heart, I was sure I hadn't given up on Nate, but I knew she still thought I had. I wanted to cry every time I saw her. Her words put a wall between us which could not be torn down easily.

> It is harder to win back the friendship of an
> offended brother than to capture a fortified
> city. His anger shuts you out like iron bars
> (Proverbs 18:19, TLB).

For those who want to comfort others, I would caution that you be sensitive. When you are talking with those who are going through trauma, allow for the work that God is doing in their hearts, and take your cue from what they say.

In our case, God was very clearly preparing us for Nathan's death even as we drove to the hospital. He was working with us and planting peace in our hearts. Those who were close to us sensed it immediately. Nate didn't die because we had "given up"; Nate died because God said, "I miss you, Nate; come on home."

It is very important to acknowledge a person's loss quickly; through a note, a card, or a personal visit, but don't feel you must explain or justify the trauma.

Of all the ways you can help those in crisis, offering "words of wisdom" can be the most risky. Even if your suggestions or philosophy are positive, they may not be accepted in a positive manner by those who are in the middle of a trauma.

Dr. Henry Brandt has been my personal friend for over thirty years, and we have been through many trials together. I trust him and often ask for his counsel. Uncle Henry, as I fondly call him, spent the weekend with us after Nate's death. I was glad he came.

Each time I began to get upset because of the circumstances we were facing, Uncle Henry would lovingly put his arm around me, hug me, and say, "Let the peace of God rule in your heart" (Colossians 3:15).

His words were scriptural — but each time he hugged me and made me the benefactor of his spiritual insight, I got angry.

I knew what he was trying to say. He was pointing out that my peace should come from Christ and not from my circumstances, but I didn't want to hear it. My son was dead; why should I want peace?

Fortunately, Dr. Brandt and I knew each other well enough so that he could risk my anger. As my anger dwindled, through Uncle Henry's words I was able once again to ask God for His peace so that I could face this December of my life victoriously.

My rule of thumb when talking to a bereaved person is: If you don't know what to say, if you aren't sure how God is working in the situation, just hug the person. Offer advice only sparingly.

If you are the one who is suffering, and if people have said things which seem insensitive or do not help or comfort when you are grieving, ask God to guide your response. It is unlikely they meant to be unkind; in fact, as in Dr. Brandt's case, they may be saying what you need to hear. Try to learn from the experience and be sensitive and compassionate as you deal with others.

Before you try to console with words, make sure you have already established a good rapport with the bereaved, and don't be offended if your advice is not immediately accepted. I'm glad Dr. Brandt was willing to take the risk, and I'm also thankful he stuck with me even when I didn't want to accept his advice.

As comforters, we should tread softly. Sometimes there isn't anything we can say except "I love you; I'm praying for you, and I'm here for you."

"From a wise mind comes careful and persuasive speech" (Proverbs 16:23, TLB).

Let me suggest some other forms of encouragement and comfort you can offer, which may minimize your risk of saying the wrong thing.

In spite of sorrow, people still need to eat, but few bereaved people have the motivation or strength to prepare meals for themselves. If you like to cook and have the time, your favorite dish will be much appreciated by a grieving family.

You don't have to be a gourmet cook to help. Shortly after breakfast on that fateful Friday morning, my friend Jackie arrived with a sack of groceries: cheese, crackers, bread, cinnamon rolls, other snacks, napkins, and paper plates. This helped tremendously.

Several years ago the teenage son of a man who served on a church board with Glen died very suddenly. I felt we should visit the family right away, but since we didn't know them well, I was a little nervous.

I took a loaf of homemade bread out of my freezer, thinking, *Even if they don't want to see us, they'll like my bread.* We went to their door armed with my bread. A friend of the family welcomed us, accepted the bread, and invited us in.

We found the family and their close friends so dazed by the circumstances surrounding the boy's death that no one seemed able to think about what needed to be done. I asked, "Has the pastor been called?"

"No."

"Have friends been called?"

"No."

No plans had been made for meals or for accommodations for relatives who would be coming from out of town.

When I asked if I could stay and help with some of those details, they readily accepted.

Glen returned home to take care of our children and I stayed until late that evening. I returned daily for the next several days to help with funeral arrangements, make phone calls, and plan meals, and the mother even asked me to help her clean out their son's room. A simple loaf of bread had opened the door and made it possible for me to see the needs and to help the family in a very vital way.

One act of kindness I particularly appreciated was when people brought pictures of Nathan which they had taken. Some were of events we had also photographed, but were different poses or groupings. Others laminated newspaper articles of the accident and funeral for us.

Several of Nathan's classmates cleaned our house the week after Nate's death. Two of them, Debbie and Julie, offered to come on a weekly basis for the remainder of the school year. What a blessing!

I am an organized person and under normal circumstances would have no trouble keeping my house clean, but during this time, cleaning a bathroom or running a vacuum were of little importance to me. I used all of the strength I had just to function at work. When I got home I collapsed into a chair. I didn't have the emotional or physical strength to do much cleaning or cooking. I am so grateful these girls saw my need and were willing to commit themselves to help.

God also had a special bonus in store for all of us through this. Two years later Debbie became my daughter-in-law! We both look back to her "housecleaning days" as a wonderful time for a future mother-in-law and daughter-in-law to get to know each other. Debbie is one of our very beautiful and special roses.

We received more than six hundred cards and letters after Nathan's death, and they still comfort me. The cards with personal notes were especially meaningful.

Many people chose to telephone us rather than to come to the house. This was fine, but often I could not talk long because of all the activity in our home, and I was sorry I couldn't reach out and hug those people.

Some people sent telegrams of condolences and we appreciated their thoughtfulness. We also appreciated the flowers and plants which were sent to the house. I have been able to keep most of the plants alive and they are a lovely reminder of those who grieved with us.

You can help a bereaved person in many different ways. It's best for you to be sensitive and ask God to open your eyes to the ways most natural for you.

The evening after the accident was our school's first homecoming event. Nate and the other boy injured in the accident both played trumpet in the pep band. How can a pep band be peppy without trumpets? Helen, a mother of students at the school, and an accomplished trumpet player, asked herself that question and came up with a solution.

She stopped by our house and said, "If you'll give me Nate's music, I would like to play the trumpet for him tonight at Homecoming if it's OK with you." Helen found a unique way to help in our time of need.

I recently attended the funeral of another young man killed by a drunk driver. Someone had put together a photo album of pictures portraying Tim's life. In addition, a collage of pictures was displayed on an easel — beautiful memories for us all to enjoy. What a special tribute.

Tim left a six-month-old son who didn't have time to collect memories of his daddy. As we entered the viewing room at the funeral home, a nicely printed note was placed on a table along with blank pages of paper. The note asked us to write about a memory we had of Tim. These were to be placed in a notebook to be given to Tim's son when he is old enough to appreciate it. That notebook will give the son a much-needed link to the father he never knew.

After my friend Barbara's house burned in a Southern California fire, she recalled:

> One friend went through her entire house and boxed up a wide assortment of things that she felt she would need if she had nothing. She brought items from shampoo and bobby pins to towels and face cloths and even flannel pajamas for my husband.

> At Christmas one young man brought an umbrella, jigsaw puzzles for our family, and tools for my husband.

> One dear lady who is extremely shy came by with some lovely clothes (some brand new) in the exact size I needed, and when she was gone we discovered rolls and a pie and all sorts of other special things. I'm not sure she ever said a word, but we will never forget what her actions said.

When another friend and her children were trying to recover from an unexpected and unwanted divorce, she greatly appreciated the families who invited her children on outings with them. She also recalls how often she wished for someone to do needed repairs around the house or simple maintenance work on the car.

I have one I-wish-we-would-have-done-that sugges-
tion. It would have been helpful later if we had had
a guest book at our home to record the names of friends who came or brought in food. Several hundred
people came through our home that week, and I wish
I had a way of remembering all of them.

I also wish someone could have helped us think in
those hours just after Nate's death. Glen and I both
regret we weren't able to donate some of Nate's organs
to a needy person, and we are sorry we didn't ask to
see Nate at the hospital after he died. Now we realize
that neither of us had been convinced absolutely that
it was really Nate until we saw his body in the casket.
We had both wanted to see him at the hospital, but
weren't able to verbalize our thoughts.

When you are with the bereaved, be a good listener.
Encourage them to express themselves freely. Don't
reprove them for what they say or feel, but help them
voice their feelings, and try to understand them. We
often tend to stay away when friends hurt because we
can think of no specific way to help. I discovered, after
Nathan's death, that the little things meant as much
as the big things. Even when we are in the midst of
grief ourselves, we can be a rose to others around us
who are hurting if we are willing to be sensitive to
their needs.

The Rose of Forgiveness

Let all bitterness, and wrath, and anger, and clamour, and evil speaking, be put away from you, with all malice: And be ye kind one to another, tenderhearted, forgiving one another, even as God for Christ's sake hath forgiven you (Ephesians 4:31,32).

H ave you forgiven him yet?"

"How do you feel about him?"

These were the questions people asked the first days after our son was killed by a drunk driver. At the time, the easiest thing to say was, "I don't know how I feel about him." I was trying to cope with Nate's death. I couldn't deal with the driver right then.

That answer got me through the first few weeks, but then I started asking myself the same questions.

"How *do* I feel about him? Have I forgiven him?"

I was afraid to meet him face to face because I didn't
know how I felt. What would I do when I had to see
the man who killed my son, the man who had robbed
us of the privilege of watching Nate grow up?

When I learned the accident had been caused by a
drunk driver, anger had overwhelmed me, but I remembered that I had those feelings of anger when Ethan
died. At that time my anger wasn't directed toward a
drunk driver — my anger was directed toward God. I
felt I had been "done in" by God. I had trusted Him
and told Him He could do His will in Ethan's life.
Instead of healing Ethan, He had let him die.

My anger simmered into bitterness until I read a
statement from Dr. S. I. McMillan's book, *None of
These Diseases.*

> The moment I start hating a man, I become
> his slave. I can't work any more because he
> even controls my thoughts. My resentments
> produce too many stress hormones in my
> body and I become fatigued after only a few
> hours of work. The work I formerly enjoyed
> is now drudgery. . . .
>
> The man I hate hounds me wherever I go.
> I can't escape his tyrannical grasp on my
> mind.[1]

My anger and hatred hadn't been focused on a
person, but on a situation. I was angry because Ethan
was dead, and that anger was controlling me. It was
many months after reading this before I was able to
confess my anger as sin and ask the Lord to help me
be content in my situation.

When I learned Nathan had been killed by a drunk
driver, those same feelings of anger and hatred welled
up within me. I didn't want to be a slave to anger
again, so I immediately asked God to remove those

feelings and give me victory in the midst of this terrible situation. However, my prayer was not put to the test until the time I met the man who was responsible, face to face.

As I entered the second-floor hallway the first day we were to appear in court, I saw a man sitting in a wheelchair. I just knew he must be the one. As I walked closer to the wheelchair, it turned, and I saw the man's face. He looked like a very frightened man — not a killer at all.

I didn't feel angry, nor did I want to scream or lash out at him — I just stood and let the tears fall. God had removed the bitterness and was allowing me to forgive this man.

Besides forgiveness, I also felt relief when I saw the man's face — relief that I was Nate's mother rather than this man's mother. I sensed that sin had caused this man's heartache, and I was relieved that Nate had never brought us heartache, shame or grief during all his seventeen years. We weren't having to help our child work through the guilt he would experience at causing someone else's death.

In the January 1985 issue of *Family Life Today,* Lewis Smedes identifies four stages of forgiving.

> The first stage is hurt: When somebody causes you pain so deep and unfair that you cannot forget it, you are pushed into the first stage of the crisis of forgiving.
>
> The second stage is hate: You cannot shake the memory of how much you were hurt, and you cannot wish your enemy well. You sometimes want the person who hurt you to suffer as you are suffering.
>
> The third stage is healing: You are given eyes to see the person who hurt you in a

new light. Your memory is healed, you turn back the flow of pain and are free again.

The fourth stage is the coming together: You invite the person who hurt you back into your life; if he or she comes honestly, love can move you both toward a new and healed relationship. The fourth stage depends on the person you forgive as much as it depends on you; sometimes he doesn't come back and you have to be healed alone.[2]

Nate died in February but I didn't see the driver of the other car until several months later. God needed all of that time to prepare my heart and get me ready to be forgiving.

I went through all of the stages that Mr. Smedes mentioned. The hurt I felt seemed unbearable. Nate was gone. I would never see him on this earth again, and I was completely broken. A total stranger had caused us this relentless, throbbing pain and totally disrupted our lives.

Although I didn't actually hate the man, I hated the fact that he could throw us into such chaos and still walk around free, seemingly unscathed.

The summer after Nate's death, I was trying to locate a friend's home, and I got lost. I looked up at the street sign and realized I was on the street where the man lived who had killed Nate. I didn't want to be there, but before I could find a place to turn around, I saw him playing ball with his son.

After I turned the corner, I parked the car and cried. I hated it that he — the man who killed my son — could enjoy a summer afternoon with his son. He robbed me of a privilege he was still experiencing. Oh, how I wished he could feel my devastation and my sorrow.

The beginning of healing came when I met him in the courtroom because I was able to see him in a new light, not only as the man who had come crashing into our lives, who had seemed to have little regard for our feelings, but I was able to see him also as a frightened, needy man.

Because of the legal circumstances there has been no "coming together." I have experienced my healing alone. Although I have never been able to share my feelings with the man who caused Nate's death, God has healed me enough so that I am able to pray that God will bring him peace.

As Christians, we mistakenly expect all victims to be ready to offer instant forgiveness to those who have hurt them. A friend came to me the morning after Nathan died and asked me to go to the hospital to tell the driver of the other car I had forgiven him. In the middle of the night Glen and I had called the hospital chaplain, who is a friend of ours, and asked him to see the man as soon as possible, but I was not ready to meet him face to face.

Another acquaintance was so insistent I display forgiveness immediately, she sent a card to the man, signing our family's name along with hers, stating, "We love you and forgive you."

I could have gone to the hospital immediately, or quickly sent a card proclaiming forgiveness, but in my case it would have been premature.

When we are grieving, we shouldn't feel compelled to rush forgiveness. It may be necessary to allow time for the situation to sink in and for God to do a work in our hearts. If you are the one who is grieving, be open to God's guiding and allow Him to lead you in the direction of forgiveness. I am not condoning vengeance or uncontrolled anger, but you may find there is a neutral stage where you have no feelings one way or the other; you are numb. The neutral stage can be a provision from God to protect you from feelings of grief or anger which would be too great for you to control. Forgiveness, especially in a traumatic or crisis situation, will take time. Give God time.

Although God helped me control the feelings of bitterness and anger toward the drunk driver, I allowed myself to get tripped up in another area.

Because all of the teenagers in Nathan's car came from Christian families, I hoped we would be able to work together in harmony. However, we had difficulty agreeing about anything. Because of this, the insurance settlement, which we had hoped would happen in sixty to ninety days, took fifteen months — months of problems and hurt feelings. And my bitterness grew.

I knew God could help me overcome these feelings, but I didn't want His help. I preferred to sit and stew. Why couldn't the other families understand we needed to get all of the legal matters behind us? It was as though we were waiting for the benediction at the funeral. We couldn't make decisions on our own, and we couldn't control our schedule. And every time I thought I was beginning to learn to handle things, we would get a call from an attorney or the insurance company, and it would start all over again. I was angry at the situation and at the people who were "allowing everything to drag on so long."

When I saw the other families, my hands shook; and when they called, I cried. I was allowing my anger to dictate my reactions to everything and everyone around me.

One day when the anger was boiling especially hot inside of me, I received a note from a friend. It said, "Marilyn, I don't understand everything that you're going through, but I have one thought I would like to share with you. 'Keep the wound clean.'"

What timing! I burst into tears as I cried out to God for help. I had not kept the wound clean but had allowed it to fester with so much bitterness. As I confessed my sin to the Lord, I asked Him to forgive me and help me cleanse the wound of anything which would keep it from healing properly: the anger, the bitterness, the frustration, the impatience. The desire for these attitudes to leave came immediately, but it took, and still takes, lots of work and determination to keep the festering from beginning again. I have spent much time in study and prayer, asking God to help me "keep the wound clean."

Joni Eareckson Tada's book, *A Step Further,* helped me to look at our situation from others' points of view and to learn to forgive others. Joni explains:

> It's a kind of scale, I finally reasoned. Every person alive fits somewhere onto a scale of suffering that ranges from little to much.
>
> And it's true. Wherever we happen to be on that scale — that is, however much suffering we have to endure — there are always those below us who suffer less, and those above who suffer more. The problem is we usually like to compare ourselves only with those who suffer less. That way we can pity ourselves and pretend we're at the top of the scale. But when we face reality and stand beside those who suffer more, our purple-heart medals don't shine so brightly.[3]

God let me see I had become pious about my suffering. After all, how many people do you know who have lost three children? I placed myself rather high on the scale of suffering; surely no one had suffered more than I had.

God rebuked me for my attitude and showed me many people who have suffered more. At first I resisted the idea, but I finally had to admit I didn't know what

it was like to be a Joni Eareckson, confined to a wheelchair for the rest of my life, or to suffer through a
divorce, or sit by the bed of a child who was in a
coma. Many people were experiencing griefs greater
than mine.

I had to ask God to forgive me for my self-righteous
attitudes and to help me show compassion toward
those who are suffering, whether or not their problems
seem of great significance to me.

As I did this, God began to give me a greater compassion toward those with whom I had been angry.
Perhaps they were experiencing the same thing I had
experienced. From their position on the scale of suffering, they also might be having a hard time realizing
that someone else could suffer more than they. I began
to pray for them daily, that God would supply their
needs, and give them peace and understanding. I
prayed the same prayer for myself. A short time later,
one of the families came to us and asked our forgiveness
for their lack of understanding and compassion.

God does hear and answer our prayers, but many
times the work has to begin with us. As I asked God
to remove the roots of bitterness, He answered my
prayer and replaced those bitter roots with roots of
love and compassion.

God is kind in that He doesn't dump all of our
faults on us at once. He knows how much we can
handle at one time. God gave me the desire to forgive
the drunk driver; then, many months later, He gently
showed me that my attitude toward the other families
was wrong and I obediently confessed my sin.

Nearly three years after Nate's death, I participated
in a communion service with a small group of people.
The leader suggested we ask God to show us any sin
in our lives regarding the other people in the room,
then with family members, and finally with others
with whom we associated. As I prayed, I felt no problem

with anyone in the group nor with my family, but as my thoughts moved on to others, God stopped me short.

I could hear the voice of the lady who told me, "Nate is dying because you have given up." I tried to reason, "But Lord, she's the one who needs forgiving; I didn't do anything wrong." Instantly, God allowed me to see the bitterness that I had harbored against her. As I asked God to forgive me, a great load lifted from me, and then I was free to forgive my friend. God knew when I was able to deal with that sin and He did not confront me with it until that time.

If you have a friend who is struggling with forgiving someone, don't condemn him for his feelings. The best thing you can do is to serve as a sounding board and pray him through the forgiving process.

If you are hurting because someone has caused you a deep and unfair pain and you have been pushed into the "crisis stage" of forgiving, give yourself time. Give God time.

Your responsibility is to make sure you don't allow the wound to fester with anger and bitterness. Keep the wound clean. Stay open with God. He will lead you into forgiveness.

As you offer the rose of forgiveness to someone else, you will receive your own rose, that great gift of freedom from the bondage of anger and bitterness.

The Rose
of
Remembrance

I thank my God upon every remembrance of you (Philippians 1:3).

Glen and I are members of Compassionate Friends, a support group for bereaved parents. Each month, as newly-bereaved parents come, they ask similar questions:

"Why don't people mention his name?"

"Why don't they talk about him?"

"Have they forgotten him already?"

Non-bereaved friends say, "We don't want to remind you of your loss or give you added grief, so it seems better not to talk about your child any more."

In Joe Bayly's book, *The Last Thing We Talk About,* Mr. Bayly writes that his little girl described her feelings about her brother's impending death as being "like something is pinned to the front of your mind all the time."[1]

Most people who have lost a loved one will agree with her. Everything else that goes into our mind has to be filtered through the thought, *My wife (or my husband or my child) is dead.*

Rarely will you remind family members of something they are not already thinking about. You can be sure they will remember birthdays, the anniversaries of the death, and most assuredly the events which led up to the death.

The week of Nate's crash I had been very busy working on student aid applications, along with a national scholarship application that was due that week.

As a counselor, I did those things the same month of each year. For two or three years after the accident I still got very depressed when I started working on those applications. It was as if I were heading toward the crash again, and it helped when people acknowledged that that time of year must be hard for me.

Some people say, "I don't want to mention it because I may cause you more hurt." I am going to hurt whether they mention it or not because I can't get away from reminders; they are all around me. When friends mention the anniversary date is coming up, they *are* reminding me of the accident, but they're also reminding me they are hurting with me. They're supporting me, and they care for me.

Although friends may mean well, their avoidance of talking about the one who has died can hurt the bereaved family deeply. I talk about Nate often because I enjoy talking about him. Acknowledging his existence helps keep him alive in my mind, and right now it is important to me to remember the normal, natural, human things about him.

From my loss of Jimmy and Ethan, I realize memories do fade. I didn't have either of those babies long enough to have many memories. Now, twenty years later, I can barely picture their faces. When Nate died, I began to fear that in a few years I wouldn't be able to remember him clearly, so I asked for a special gift from the Lord. I prayed I would always be able to see an image in my mind of Nate alive, and I would be able to remember the sound of his voice. God granted my request in a unique and special way.

Shortly after the accident we learned Nate's coach had video-taped a basketball game less than two weeks before Nate died. On that tape, Nate is real. He directs traffic as he dribbles the ball down the court and he puts his arm around the coach as the coach gives him some new piece of strategy. I can see him pat another player on the back as he enters the game, and he even makes six points. Whenever I watch the tape, I still find myself cheering for him when he makes a good play. My memory of Nate alive is preserved forever on that tape.

More than two and a half years after Nate's death, I started to play a cassette tape of myself which I had recorded when I was speaking at a luncheon a few months earlier. I inadvertently placed the tape into the recorder on the wrong side. I listened to the woman speaking and thought, *Who is that? That isn't my voice.*

As I listened, I heard a piano and a male voice. I quickly realized I had discovered a tape of one of Nathan's voice lessons! I prayed, "Oh God, please let me hear him clearly; don't tease me with this." As he began to sing, the teacher suggested he move closer to her, which was also closer to the tape recorder. I could hear him perfectly. God answered my prayer!

I sat on the floor of our living room sobbing as I heard Nate sing one song and discuss it with his teacher. She asked, "Nate do you have any more songs?"

He answered, "I've got one more. It isn't my favorite, but it's my mom's favorite and I want to learn it for her!"

I felt I had moved back in time, back to when things were normal, back when I couldn't comprehend how much emotional pain one body could stand. I hungrily devoured each precious note as Nate sang the beautiful Jewish melody, "Pierce My Ear, O Lord."

When Nate finished, the teacher said, "Nate, that was beautiful. I understand why your mom likes that song."

In his typical phlegmatic fashion, Nate said, "Yeah, not much melody, but kind of mellow."

Can you possibly imagine the joy I felt as I listened to my Nate sing? It was like a special delivery letter from heaven. More than two years after Nate's death, God answered my request that I would never forget the sound of his voice.

Most people want to talk about their deceased loved one, they hunger for even small reminders, and they want you, as their friends, to help them keep the memory of that person alive. One bereaved parent stated, "A person's not dead until he's forgotten."

Obviously, this is an area where you must be sensitive. Let the bereaved person set the pace. If he changes the subject when you mention the deceased's name, he may be trying to tell you that it hurts too much to talk about his loss. Just follow his lead.

Jean, a recently bereaved parent, related that her co-workers told her of customers who stood at the counter and wept when they heard of her son Joe's death. However, when Jean came back to work, those same customers could not talk with her about Joe.

One day she was chatting with a customer about haircuts, and she mentioned Joe always got a haircut every two weeks. When Jean mentioned Joe's name, the customer said, "Oh, that's nice," and hurriedly left the shop. How much better if he just could have touched her hand and said, "It's so good you can talk about Joe freely. You know, I miss him, too."

Nate was a cross-country runner. The fall after he died, many of his close friends were on the cross-country team at school. Christian, one of Nate's best friends, asked me to come and watch them run. I enjoyed the meet, but as the runners crossed the finish line, my mind flashed back to the previous year when Nate placed high enough to qualify for the league finals. A few tears slipped down my cheeks, but I wasn't embarrassed because I looked up and saw Christian's father had tears in his eyes also. He came over, put his arm around me, and said, "I'm thinking about him, too."

Many of Nate's friends wrote me notes with little stories about him. Sue, one of his classmates, wrote:

> One of the things that I continue to be thankful for is the precious memories I have of Nate. I miss walking through the halls and singing with Nate. He always had a song that he would share. He often asked me how he could help when no one else knew I was down. He carried my burdens. He was and is a dear friend. I just wanted you to share my thankfulness.

I dreaded the approach of June of 1984 because Nate would have graduated then. At baccalaureate the students presented a slide show of Nathan which they had compiled, with a tape of B. J. Thomas singing "Home Where I Belong" as background music. After the program they presented the slides and tape to me with this note:

Dear Mrs. Heavilin,

This slide show in no way expressed all that Nathan was to us or to you; but, in a way, the words of the song, "Home Where I Belong," expressed our security in the fact that we will see Nate again.

We also pray that this little token of our love for Nate will continually remind you of our support for you and your family.

Nathan was an irreplaceable part of our class; but Nathan is home where he belongs.

With all our love in Him, the class of 1984.

As the school counselor, it was my job to present all of the scholarships and awards at the graduation ceremonies. I prayed God would dry up my seemingly never-ending well of tears as I prepared for that event.

Each year the seniors give roses to their parents during the ceremony. As a faculty member, I handed the roses to the students so they could take them to their parents.

Many thoughts flooded my mind as I passed a flower to each student. *One of these should be mine. I wonder how Nate would give it to me. He would probably do something silly. He might be giggling.* Most of all, I was thinking, *I want a rose. I feel cheated and left out.*

After the students had returned to the platform, I saw two of the seniors walking toward me with a bouquet of roses and I was instantly overwhelmed! Their thoughtfulness assured me they cared for me and they missed Nate, too. God allowed me to see He was working in those teenagers' lives. He was making them more serious than most students would be on graduation night, and they were learning compassion through Nate's death.

Their action released both me and the audience to cry together. If I had fallen apart while making the scholarship presentations, I would have been crying alone in front of an audience. But their kind gesture made my loss public enough so that it was acceptable for us all to cry together. After a minute or so, we regained our composure and were able to proceed with the ceremony. Acknowledgment of my grief was very important to me because it gave me courage to go on.

When others acknowledge that a situation might be hard, it often bolsters people to bravery. But when the bereaved are placed in a situation which is going to be difficult, and everyone goes on as if nothing has happened, it is much harder for them to keep their composure.

Parents at Compassionate Friends have shared that family times are particularly difficult for them because few people are willing to acknowledge that a member of the family is missing. Many bereaved parents stop seeing their families at Christmas or other traditional holidays for this reason. Families think they are helping by not mentioning the deceased child, but the bereaved parents are being torn apart inside.

Our family traditionally celebrated Christmas on Christmas Eve, and because that was also Aunt Lucille's birthday, we always made it a double celebration. But after Aunt Lucille and Uncle Louie, mom's sister and brother-in-law, died as a result of the explosion and flash fire, Mom wanted to cancel December, too. However, Christmas had to come.

A friend of my mother's sent her a poem that expressed all our feelings. My mom put the poem in with a box of pictures and tucked it away. This past December I was sorting through that box and found the poem. What timing!

Once again Christmas, a birthday, and the loss of a loved one were all mixed together. The poem was appropriate, even thirty-five years later, so I made copies of it and sent it to other bereaved friends.

"MERRY" CHRISTMAS

I question if Christmas can ever be "merry,"
Except to the heart of an innocent child —
For when time has taught us the meaning of sorrow
And sobered the spirits that once were so wild,

When all the green graves that lie scattered behind us
Like milestones are marking the length of the way,
And echoes of voices that no more shall greet us
Have saddened the chimes of the bright
Christmas Day —

We may not be merry, the long years forbid it,
The years that have brought us such manifold smarts,
But we may be happy, if only we carry
The Spirit of Christmas deep down in our hearts.

Hence I shall not wish you the old "Merry Christmas,"
Since that is of shadowless childhood a part,
But one that is holy and happy and peaceful,
The Spirit of Christmas deep down in your heart.

— Author Unknown

My daughter and her husband did something very special to help us through our first Christmas after Nate died. Since Nate's birthday was Christmas Day, I was apprehensive about it all. I invited many of our friends to spend the day with us and I claimed the promise I had discovered many months before that God would give us "roses in December."

Christmas morning, my son-in-law Mike showed me a card he placed on the Christmas tree. It was addressed to Nate, but Mike handed it to me.

Dear Family,

Mellyn and I wanted to do something special this Christmas in thanksgiving to our Father for His incredible blessings upon us.

It is our desire, if the Lord wills, to establish a tradition of Christmastime giving — a real sacrifice of ourselves for others, in memory of Nathan.

Mike and Mellyn

The first year they took a basket of food to a needy family and told the family they were doing this in memory of their brother, Nathan. This past year, they helped a Vietnamese family. A remembrance like that is a rose, a very special rose in December.

We have adopted the same custom, and each year at Christmas we choose a boy to send to basketball camp in memory of Nate. This year, our friends, Nancy and Peter, sent a contribution to a Christian organization in Nate's name.

I am thankful for the friends who have stuck with us during these difficult years. Undoubtedly there were times when they were tired of hearing about Nate, the accident, the trial, the insurance, etc. They probably wondered if we would ever stop talking about him, but they were patient and they let us talk. It was a very important part of our healing.

We don't talk about Nate constantly now. We are beginning to see him as "one of the children," not necessarily just as the "one who died."

Our friends have learned to talk about him in a natural way, too. We can laugh about his funny and sometimes irritating habits, the times he did something wrong, his pet peeves, and all of the fun we had with him. He is beginning to take a normal spot in the history of the Heavilin family. Much of this normality has been regained because our friends have given us freedom to talk about him and work through our loss. They have also taken time to remember with us, for which we will be forever grateful.

If you have experienced a recent loss, let me encourage you to find friends with whom you can talk freely. Support groups can be helpful also. Perhaps there is a group in your church which can meet your needs. If not, try to find a group such as Compassionate Friends. Although they do not have a Christian emphasis, you will find there other people who will understand your feelings and your frustrations.

If you have friends or co-workers with whom you feel strained because you can't share how you really feel, don't be too hard on them. If they are close friends, gently explain your needs. If they still don't respond, try to understand that their background and training may not free them to be as open as you would like them to be. Love them anyway, and let them learn from you. Perhaps they will observe enough so that they will be able to pass your attitudes on to others even if they can't help you.

Thank God for all of the friends He gives you who do understand. They are beautiful, priceless roses.

The Rose of Friendship

A true friend is always loyal, and a brother is born to help in time of need (Proverbs 17:17, TLB).

W hen I was a little girl, my father had a plaque hanging in his office which read, "He is rich who has two friends." After Nathan's death, God showed me that regarding friends, I was a millionaire!

Most people going through a tragedy have more help than they need the first week or so. But soon the crowd thins out. The bereaved often ask, "Where are all of those people who said they would help me?"

I was afraid that would happen in our case, but it didn't. Oh, of course, the crowd thinned out, but we had many people who stuck with us.

When Nate died, my friend Donna Lynn was expecting her sixth child. She didn't have a lot of time to come to my house or take me to lunch, but her limited time didn't keep her from helping me. She helped by letting me help her.

She would call and say, "Marilyn, I need some typing done [or someone to watch the baby, or someone to be outside with her four-year-old]. Will you come and help me?" After I helped her, we would have some time to talk. Donna Lynn accomplished two things with this approach. She helped me feel useful again and showed she cared by spending quality time with me. I'm glad she didn't let her busy schedule get in the way of helping a friend.

I didn't know Joan well before the accident, although her children were close friends of Nate's. That didn't stop her from coming to our house the very first morning and cooking breakfast for us.

A few weeks later at church, Joan said, "Marilyn, I just want to tell you how much I appreciate it that you're letting the people in this church watch you grieve. You are open with how we can help you. You aren't trying to hide your feelings from us. We're a new church, and we need to learn how to work with people in crisis."

Then she went on to ask, "Would you be willing to meet me for lunch periodically so I can learn more from you?"

Her psychology was wonderful. She could have said, "Let me take you to lunch so that I can help you, honey." But she didn't. She put me in a position where I felt comfortable accepting her invitation. She didn't make me feel like a charity case.

When I accepted her offer, I had no idea of all we would be facing in the next few months. Many times I got so frustrated with the legal system, or the insurance situation, that I would think to myself, *If I can just hang on until Wednesday when I have lunch with Joan, I'll be OK.*

I knew I could be honest with Joan. I didn't have to be guarded about what I said. I could trust her with my deepest feelings. Through those very difficult months, Joan was my release valve. She helped me keep my sanity and a proper perspective on the situation.

During one of those lunches, Joan shared how Nate's death had affected her family. Her daughters Sue and Donna were so moved by his death that just going to the funeral, paying their respects, and helping us didn't seem like enough. As a family, they decided to do something which would involve them personally. For several weeks their family had a moratorium on television in memory of Nate. They felt if the whole country could do so in honor of a deceased president, the Morrill family could certainly curtail their television watching in honor of a friend.

Their act of sacrifice was very kind, but it meant even more because they shared it with us. The bereaved are encouraged when they know their loss is shared by others.

My friend Nancy was the first person we called after we heard about the accident. She came to the hospital immediately — a thermos of coffee in hand — and then came home with us and stayed until midnight Friday evening. Nancy and her husband Pete practically lived with us for the next two or three weeks.

Nancy made all of the phone calls we couldn't make; she helped arrange for food to be brought in; and she took care of our guests. Pete handled the logistics of such things as getting people from one place to another and bringing chairs from the church to our house after the funeral.

A few weeks later I discovered Nancy had done something even more special as she handed me a legal-sized note pad and a cassette tape. She said, "Here's the start of your book whenever you decide to write about this."

She went on to explain she had been taking notes for the past few weeks of everything that had been going on at our house; the people, the phone calls, the gifts, the cards, and our reactions. Then she had made a cassette tape of her personal feelings about Nate's death.

It was a long time before I could listen to the tape, and it was hard to imagine I would ever forget the details of those two weeks. But as I read the notes and listened to the tape about six months later, I discovered I had already forgotten much of what had happened. As time passes, I realize more and more how special Nancy's gift really was.

The best thing some of my friends did for me was just to let me cry. Sometimes, the minute I would hear a friend's voice, I would start to cry. My friends didn't condemn me; they simply let me cry.

My friend Diana is very sensitive to my needs, and she can tell when I am getting ready for a good cry. When I call and ask if she can meet me at my favorite restaurant for a piece of pie, she doesn't question me. She just says, "What time?" It is so comfortable to be with Diana because she freely admits she misses Nate, too. She doesn't just watch me cry; she cries with me. That's a true friend.

On the second anniversary of Nate's homegoing, my mother took flowers to the grave. She found a bouquet already there with a card which read, "Nate, we'll never forget you. See you later." It was from Diana and her family. Diana is a special rose in our bouquet of December roses.

Friends can be sensitive to the needs of children in bereaved families by giving them extra attention, taking them places, or just listening to them. Frequently, the parents are so distraught themselves they are oblivious to the needs of the children.

Our son Matt had sat with his friend Roger the November before Nate's death when Roger's wife faced serious surgery. He carried food to Roger, ran errands for him, and was his sounding board. After Nate's crash, Roger was able to return the favor to Matt. He came to the hospital and then stuck with Matt during the remainder of the day.

In Matt's words, Nate had been his "social life" for several years. He had transported Nate and his friends to many high school events and even had driven them on the field trip to Los Angeles the day of the accident.

Roger recognized the empty space that Matt would need to fill and he helped by spending as much time with him as possible in the early weeks following the accident. Often bereaved brothers and sisters are forgotten, so we are grateful that Roger saw he could minister to Matt just by being there.

Our pastor was a special friend to us. Pastors often *want* to spend time with bereaved families, but their schedules won't allow for daily or weekly calls, and the families seem to get lost in the pool of good intentions. Our pastor found a way to keep in touch with us without spending a lot of time. The greatest thing he did was come as soon as we called. The week of the funeral he stopped by daily, but after that he called us each evening between 9 and 10. We both got on the phone for a three-way conversation with him which enabled us to hear each other's reaction to his questions.

He would ask, "How did it go today?" We would relate the happenings of the day.

"How do you feel about today's happenings?" Sometimes we felt good, and sometimes we didn't. Often we would shed a few tears with him.

"What's happening tomorrow?" We would relate our plans; perhaps we had a special meeting or a court date.

"Let's pray." We would join in conversational prayer for the events of the next day.

"Now go to bed and get some rest." Often we went to bed simply because he suggested it. Sometimes we didn't seem able to make even those simple decisions for ourselves.

Those conversations usually took only five to ten minutes, but they met a vital need in our lives. The pastor communicated that he cared, and he also sensed if we had some special needs the church could meet.

In a large church, the pastor probably would not be able to make contact through a daily phone call, but he could assign an elder, deacon, deaconess, or another caring person to keep in touch with the family and serve as a link to himself and to the church.

A pastor's secretary could keep a card file, with notations such as: "Nate Heavilin died February 11, 1983; send Glen and Marilyn a card." This special touch would be greatly appreciated by the bereaved family.

Occasionally during the next few months a note would appear in our bulletin, "Remember to pray for the Heavilins as they continue to adjust to their recent loss." Our pastor was giving us time to grieve.

Although people want to help the bereaved, many times they don't because they simply don't know what to do. We had to be willing to make our needs known. Sometimes this was hard because we didn't want to admit we needed other people. But when we did, we found most people willing, and even anxious, to help us.

There were days when the depression was so heavy I didn't have the strength to pick up the phone and call so someone could encourage me.

On those days, I cried out to God and said, "God, I think I need help. If You agree with me, please have someone call me or contact me because I just don't have the strength to reach out to anyone today. If no one calls, then I'll know that You want me to work through this alone with You. I will trust You to meet my needs in the right way."

My prayer has always been answered, and I have received many calls from people stating, "I don't know why I'm calling, but God just kept bringing you to my mind, so I had to call to see how you're doing."

Other times I didn't receive any calls, but God would show me a Scripture or lead me to a book, or give me a special thought that would lift my spirits and help me go on with life.

My friend Irene lives in Chicago, more than two thousand miles away, but she and I have become very sensitive to each other's needs.

One day I felt a strong desire to call Irene. I tried several times, but no one was home. When I finally reached her late that evening, Irene heard my voice and burst into tears. She sobbed, "Oh Marilyn, Jonathan [her only child] is in the hospital and we don't know what's wrong with him."

After Irene shared more details with me, we were able to pray together and claim God's peace for Irene, Jonathan, and the rest of the family. Irene received comfort in the realization that if God cared enough about her to touch the heart of a friend thousands of miles away, then surely He was aware of Jonathan's needs and would care for him, too.

When God puts someone on your mind, respond right away. God is most likely wanting to use you to respond to that person's immediate need. If you can't call or go to them, then at least take time to pray for them, asking God to meet their needs as He sees fit.

A friend will not force himself on those in need, but will be responsive to their needs. A faithful friend is a beautiful rose.

If you are the bereaved person, be willing to let your needs be known. When you're having a terrible day, don't be afraid to admit it. Call somebody and just say, "Help." If you are so discouraged you don't have the strength to ask for help from other people, remember God has promised He will always be with you.

> The Lord is nigh unto them that are of a broken heart; and saveth such as be of a contrite spirit (Psalm 34:18).

Call on Him. He will hear, and He will answer. He wants to be your forever friend.

The Rose of Understanding

How much better is wisdom than gold, and understanding than silver (Proverbs 16:16, TLB).

W hen Nathan died, I felt compelled to get back immediately into my regular routines at work, at home, and in my social life. It seemed that continuing on in all of my previous patterns could shut out the fact he was gone, as if his death were a dream or a mistake. I thought repeating normal patterns would make me feel normal again.

So, less than two weeks after Nate died, I returned to my job at the high school where he had attended. The trip to school, Nate's and my private time together, had always been so much fun. Now, making the drive alone was horrible. I tried to listen to tapes, but I couldn't retain what I heard. The traffic made me nervous, and I felt nauseous as I drove past the wrecking lot where Nate's crushed car was stored.

Being at school seemed so strange: I had lost track of my purpose for being there. I walked into my office and all I could see was the chair where Nate had sat each morning. Since teachers had to arrive early, Nate usually studied in my office before school started. As I would look into my room from the doorway after the teachers' meeting, I could see this lanky boy, sprawled comfortably in a chair, his size-eleven feet propped on another chair. When I returned to work, that scene, still vivid in my mind, haunted me.

The first day back, I learned that two of my students had received highly coveted scholarships, the very ones I had worked on so enthusiastically the day of Nate's accident. Hearing they had won, I burst into uncontrollable sobbing. Two weeks earlier I would have been elated; of course, I was still happy for them, but my heart was breaking because as his counselor I would never get a chance to help my Nate win a scholarship. After two hours of trying to work, I went home.

Occasionally I tried to write my feelings:

> The fog still hasn't lifted. I move, I walk, I talk, but it is all automatic. There is little feeling. Sometimes the fog lifts and the feelings rush in. Then, all I can do is cry. It seems the only time I am real, reacting honestly, without guarding every word or look, I start to cry.
>
> When the fog lifts for a brief moment, it is as though someone just kicked me in the stomach. As I am reeling with the pain, my mind registers the one prevailing thought: Nathan is gone; NATHAN IS GONE. When

> I can't stand the pain anymore, my mind goes
> back into neutral, back into the fog.

Although I managed to continue working for the next two years, time didn't really improve the situation. Often I felt I was stumbling around in a dream; my mind wouldn't concentrate on any one thing for more than a few minutes. The extra-curricular activities — basketball, cross-country, ensemble — lost their meaning. There were constant reminders everywhere — scholarships, graduation, homecoming. Within a few weeks everyone else was back to normal, but Glen and I finally realized we had no normal to get back to. We had to learn a new normal, a normal without Nate.

Society needs to understand what trauma is and what it (especially an unexpected, traumatic loss) does to a person. We may look all right on the outside, but our minds do not function properly, and may not for months, or even years. I related to a young mother who had just lost a six-week-old child how sometimes I could not keep a thought in my head long enough to find a piece of paper and write it down. She exclaimed, "Oh thank goodness you have that problem, too. I thought I was losing my mind!"

My friend Mary recently suffered a stroke. Although she is not paralyzed, she has only partial vision in each eye. She says, "Even though I look all right to others, on the inside I feel separated from myself. I feel very unsure of myself and need encouragement, but because I appear to be all right, people don't recognize I need help." Emotionally hurting people also may appear whole but inside they feel very fragmented. The emotional pain tends to short-circuit their thought patterns.

Parents at Compassionate Friends have shared that sometimes they are driving on the freeway and they can't remember where they're going. Others have called someone and when the person answers, they can't remember whom they were calling.

Many bereaved people change educational plans or vocational direction because they have lost the drive to go on. These situations often don't improve in the first few months; it may be years before the person can remain constant in his lifestyle.

It helps if pastors, counselors and friends understand that these reactions are normal: They can encourage the bereaved person not to give up but to try to discover if a temporary adjustment can be made. An extended leave of absence, a day off each week, or even a change to a part-time position may relieve the immediate pressure. Above all, they should help the bereaved person understand he should not feel guilty about being unable to function normally. The situation isn't normal after a death or other severe crisis, and it's OK to try to make things easier until life becomes more stable.

It's not unusual for people in crisis to feel they're in spiritual limbo. Even mature Christians may not have the mental strength to maintain normal Christian patterns.

When their only child, Robert, was killed in an automobile accident, Dick and Delores displayed amazing strength. The memorial service was honoring to the Lord and many lives were touched through it. But Delores recalls, "For three weeks after Robert's death I couldn't pray for myself but felt the power of others praying for me. After this period, I had a particularly bad day and was unable to cope. Then I realized that no one was praying, and God revealed to me that I now needed to express my own needs directly to Him."

The grief process takes a different path for each person, but it is important that he allow himself to grieve. No one who has lost a loved one is going to get a special reward in heaven for returning to normality immediately as though the person never existed. Those who handle a loss well are usually those who acknowledge their pain, admit to feelings of anger or bitterness, work through those feelings, and give themselves time to heal.

My friend Barbara discovered the importance of allowing herself to grieve through two loss experiences. She says,

> At the time our son was stillborn at full term, we were living out in the country without a single house in sight. We were relatively new in the community and, though we were attending church occasionally, our roots were not deep. The church was without a pastor also. Our son was born in the same hospital and ward where I had been working as a nurse only weeks earlier so the nurses were my co-workers. A woman from our church also delivered the same day and she and her healthy baby were across the hall. None of our family lived close by. As I look back, I realize I was still playing the role of nurse — being concerned for everyone else's feelings and stuffing my own. I even helped the staff with their charting and so everyone felt I was doing "just great." No one visited us and my husband and the funeral director attended the baby's funeral all alone. My tears (and there were many) were saved for when the door was closed and it was safe — like at night when the staff was scarce and people thought I was sleeping.
>
> Our families never discussed our loss. It was as though I had never even had a baby. My husband was extremely pleasant and kind but after a couple of weeks he too felt it was

time to move on with life — and as a result those wounds never really healed.

It wasn't until twenty-three years later and the fire in which our house burned that I really understood the grieving process, and then quite by accident. We lost everything including our pet dog. Since the fire was considered a disaster and many of our friends also lost their homes or came close to losing them, people wanted to talk. We had calls from all over the United States and many friends stopped by to visit and wanted to hear *everything*. At first I cried lots as they probed, but then it became easier and easier to handle and before long I realized that those wounds had healed well. It was OK to weep.

I also became aware of the reasons healing had not occurred those many years earlier. No one deliberately wanted to hurt us. It is just so difficult to probe and see someone struggle and keep probing. However, it is essential if healing is to occur. Apparently people are more comfortable probing about things (such as fires) as opposed to the loss of a person, and I still struggle with that.

Another difficult step for some in the healing process is cleaning out the deceased person's room and distributing his possessions. There is no particular time after the death when it is best to do this, but I can tell you what was comfortable for me.

As I mentioned in the first chapter, when Jimmy died some well-meaning friends emptied our house of all reminders of Jimmy the very first day while I was out of the house, without my knowledge or consent. I came home to discover an empty bedroom and I was enraged. I managed to conceal my feelings because I realized my friends had not intended to hurt me, but I felt they had trod on sacred ground. I needed to take care of Jimmy's things as a part of my grief work, and I needed to do it when it was comfortable for me.

When Nate died, the very next morning I knew that his new Nike's and his golf clubs should go to his brother-in-law Mike. A stuffed musical dog from his childhood went to his girl friend Sheila, and his gold monogram key ring went to Matt after we had it especially engraved on the back, "To a super brother."

A few weeks later I asked some of Nate's closest friends to come over and go through his closet and choose any clothing they would like. I gave some things to a cousin for her son and sent the remaining clothes to Goodwill. I saved Nate's sweatsuit and a cowboy suit I had made for him when he was eight — they are for our future grandchildren.

It was several months before I could go through his drawers, desk and notebooks. When the time came, I asked Mellyn to spend the day with me and help finish this heart-rending project. How or when you tackle this difficult assignment is up to you, but I would recommend you not try it alone. Find someone who shares your grief and can understand and share your memories and your tears.

As the friend of a grieving person, you may be able to identify stress points before he can. Let him know that it is all right to back away and say, "I've had enough." That's not admitting defeat; it's using good sense. Often the grieving person cannot step outside of the situation enough to recognize when he's pushing himself too far.

My son Matt met a need in my life with a solution I didn't really appreciate at the time. He noticed I had difficulty with some of the phone calls I received; such as the lady who called to tell me what a nice man the

drunk driver was and how much he liked children; or
the agent from the loan company who called to make
sure we were going to make the final payment on our
mangled Toyota, but never bothered to offer his condolences; so Matt bought me a telephone answering
machine.

I had always hated those things — I found it irritating
when I called someone only to have a little machine
talk back to me.

However, I knew Matt had done the right thing.
Some days I wasn't up to talking to anyone, and I
always seemed to have difficulty talking to the families
of the other young people who had been in the accident
or to anyone regarding the legal matters, so I decided
to try the answering machine. Just knowing who was
calling before I decided if I wanted to answer the
phone was a great relief to me. Matt helped me in a
situation where I seemed unable to help myself because
I felt an obligation always to be available to others.

When you are hurting, it takes a lot of effort to try
to help yourself, but the effort is worth it. Whether
your new venture is traveling, joining a special interest
group, or starting a project, although it won't take the
hurt away, it will get you into the mainstream of life
again, and slowly the hurt will become more bearable.

It is important to understand that the bereaved may
be in shock for a few days or a few months; they need
to grieve; and they may have trouble in their jobs and
in their family. The rose of understanding is one we
all can acquire by being observant, listening to the
bereaved, and responding to what we observe.

The interests or activities which help a bereaved
person deal with his grief may seem strange to someone
else; however, I believe bereaved people can do some
rather unusual things and still be operating within the
realm of normal. But I'm sure some of you are asking,
"How can we tell if someone has moved outside the

'normal' limits?" I am not a doctor or a psychologist so I can only share with you the observations of a lay person who has experienced a great deal of grief and has talked with many people who are grieving.

If a person refuses to acknowledge that someone is dead, keeps talking in the past or continually seems to get the past and the present confused, I believe he needs professional help. If he becomes reclusive or deeply depressed, or if he openly talks of suicide, he should begin seeing a counselor. I am reluctant to put time-lines on grief because the healing process takes different lengths of time with each person, but you should be able to observe constant improvement. Even though improvement seems to come more slowly than you would like, if there is consistent progress, the person is probably doing all right. However, the healing might be accelerated if the person were to talk with a counselor or join a support group.

Christians often hesitate to seek professional help — they feel they shouldn't need it. But frequently that is exactly what they do need. It is important to get referrals and to choose a counselor carefully. If you are the grieving person, you should call the counseling center and inquire if they have counselors who deal specifically with grief therapy before you make an appointment.

Although Glen and I did not seek professional counseling, we did find great help through Compassionate Friends, a support group for bereaved parents. This statement appeared in one of their recent newsletters:

> Our grief as parents of dead children is totally unique. Not even other bereaved parents can completely understand our grief. We are all individuals and we therefore grieve in our own very personal way. What we do have in common, though, is our loss. And that loss, no matter by what means, is very overwhelming. By our coming together we are able to

share our pain and to come to the sad realization that we are not alone. At our meetings we discover other parents whose child died by similar circumstances. This will not erase our pain, but will help to support us.

In many areas there are support groups for people who have suffered specific types of losses, such people as widows, widowers, families of suicide victims, and those whose children have died from Sudden Infant Death Syndrome. If you cannot find a group in your area, you may want to start one. Ask your pastor or the local funeral director for names of people who have had recent losses similar to yours. Call and invite them to have lunch with you or meet at your home for coffee. You very likely will find comfort in sharing your experiences and feelings with each other. You will be strengthened just by realizing you were able to help a fellow griever.

When you have experienced the death of someone close, or a divorce, or some other life-changing trauma, realize that your mind, body and emotions have to adjust to this change. Read helpful books, tell others how you feel, make adjustments in your lifestyle to ease the stress and ask God to help you learn valuable truths which you can share with others, so you, too, can be a beautiful rose of understanding to those around you.

The Rose
of
Innocence

But whoso shall offend one of these little ones which believe in me, it were better for him that a millstone were hanged about his neck, and that he were drowned in the depth of the sea (Matthew 18:6).

When a crisis comes, as adults we tend to get involved in dealing with our own grief, and many times the children in the family are put in the care of a close friend or relative until "things have returned to normal." Whether children attend the funeral or not, it is important for someone to be available to answer their questions and meet their needs.

When our Jimmy died of crib death in 1964, our daughter Mellyn was almost three years old. Jimmy's crib was in Mellyn's room. Glen went in to check on the children, and discovered the baby was dead. For

the next few minutes our attention was focused on
Jimmy. Finally, I realized that Mellyn was still in the
room, and she was huddled against the wall on her
bed. Her first words were, "I didn't hurt Jimmy."

I assured her I knew she had done nothing wrong
and told her an angel had taken Jimmy to heaven to
be with Jesus. Months later I awoke in the night aware
of a little hand moving across my face. Mellyn looked
so relieved when she saw me move, and she said, "I
just wanted to see if God took you, too." Words that
had been comforting to me had been confusing to a
three-year-old.

After Jimmy's death, Mellyn reverted to baby talk
and many babyish mannerisms. She often climbed up
on my lap and said, "I'll be your baby now." It was
two or three years before we felt Mellyn was a relaxed,
carefree little girl again.

My brother was only two when his parents died
and my parents adopted him. He can't really remember
his birth parents nor the events surrounding the
tragedy, but for many months afterward he would
scream with fear when my mother left him with anyone
else. He may not have been able to remember what
had happened, but he definitely remembered the feelings of fear when his mommy and daddy left and
never came back.

A pamphlet distributed by MADD (Mothers Against
Drunk Driving) states:

> A child of two can sense loss and suffer the
> feelings that go with loss, but he cannot
> understand what death is. The child will pick
> up on the grief and anxiety in his surround-
> ings and will need touching or holding. Ex-
> planations, however, will not be understood.
> The child this young can only understand
> that someone is present or not present.

What one does is far more important to the child this young than what one says. Generally, it is best done with large doses of tender loving care — holding, cuddling, and stroking.

A child between the ages of four to six may talk of the death of the person in the same detached way that he may talk of the death of a pet. This may be disturbing to the adults around him and their reaction may be confusing. Crying may be more out of confusion about what others are experiencing rather than the death itself.

Most commonly, seven- or eight-year-olds become fearful of death because they realize for the first time that it is real. . . . Some of their questions may indicate fears of their own death. Death can now be seen as an attacker who takes life. Although able to accept the finality of death, many of the factors of early childhood still apply. It is important for children of this age to express their sadness, anger, fear, and guilt.[1]

Mellyn was five when Ethan died and I was very concerned about how she would react since Jimmy's death had been so difficult for her. However, she surprised us all. When she was told of Ethan's death, she commented, "That's OK, I've still got Nathan!"

When my grandmother died just two months later, Mellyn heard me say how bad I felt because Grandma never got to see Nathan.

She asked, "Is Grandma in heaven?"

When I said yes, she concluded, "Well, Ethan was Nate's identical twin, so he looks just like Nate. If Grandma's in heaven, she has seen Ethan, so she knows what Nate looks like."

She played with her toys a few minutes and then asked, "Do you have another grandma in heaven?"

I said, "Yes, my Grandma Empey."

With the beautifully innocent faith of a little child, Mellyn said, "Then she can have Jimmy."

Through Mellyn's faith she allowed me to see a picture of two grandmas rocking their great-grandchildren in heaven.

I personally feel it is good for children to be involved with as much of the grief experience as they are comfortable with, but it should not be forced. One family I know has experienced the deaths of three immediate family members in the past year. After the third death, the ten-year-old child said, "I can't go to another funeral," and the parents made the wise decision to let her stay home.

When a child dies, the siblings may feel guilty because God didn't take them instead of their brother or sister since, from their point of view, he or she was the smart one or the cute one, or Mom or Dad liked him or her better. A younger child may try to take the place of an older child by assuming his responsibilities, moving into his room, or wearing his clothes. Parents need to assure this child that they like him just as he is and they don't want him to be just an imitation of someone else.

Young people also may take undeserved responsibility for the death. I met a young boy whose sister committed suicide. When the sister had attempted suicide previously, the brother had determined he was going to stay with her and watch her so that she could never try suicide again. However, one day when the boy had to leave the house for a legitimate reason, the sister took the opportunity to kill herself. My young friend was filled with self-imposed guilt, "If I had just made her go with me, this would not have happened."

The parents' reassurance was not enough in this case. The boy needed an outsider's perspective to help him work through his grief and be able to forgive himself before he could realize his sister's death was not his fault.

Sometimes the remaining child will display anger because his life has been disrupted or because all of the attention seems to be focused on the dead instead of the living. He may need help in getting the right assessment of his own importance. We also need to be careful how we talk about the deceased child. We may tend to talk only about his good qualities and not acknowledge his faults to the point that the remaining children begin to feel inferior and less important than the absent child. Being aware of this potential problem can help us avoid it.

When my aunt and uncle were burned, I was twelve. My parents considered leaving me with a babysitter while they drove to the hospital in Northern Michigan, but I begged them to take me along. I did not want to be separated from my family. If we were facing trouble, I wanted us to face it together.

We arrived at the motel late in the evening and my grandparents filled us in on the details of the accident. Grandpa took my parents to the hospital and I crawled into bed with Grandma. It was the middle of the night when Grandpa walked in and said, "Louie's dead!" I can still feel my Grandma's tears falling on me as we sat on the edge of the bed and she held me so tightly.

Early the next morning we all went to the hospital to sit with my Aunt Lucille. Everyone was allowed to go into her room except me because I was not old enough, so I sat in the waiting room alone most of the day. Frequently my father came out to give me a report. One report was: "Lucille is now unconscious; we don't think she'll live much longer." Later that afternoon, Lucille died.

When the family went to see Lucille's children in the burn ward, the doctor said I could not go. I started to cry and said, "Are they dying, too?" My mother finally convinced the doctor I needed to see the children and know they were all right. My fears were relieved when I was able to talk with the children. I am thankful my parents were honest with me but I am also glad they sensed my emotional need to see the children.

During the week of the funeral people came to the house to talk with my mom and dad and my grandparents, but I don't remember anyone talking specifically with me. When I returned to school, my teacher came up to me, put her arms around me, and asked me how I was doing. The tears flooded my eyes and she held me while I sobbed. I finally felt free to express my grief.

A bereaved sibling who attended Compassionate Friends stated, "This is the first time anyone has asked, 'What happened to you?' Finally, someone has acknowledged that my brother's death didn't just happen to my parents; it happened to me, too."

Take time to seek out the children in a bereaved family. If they don't want to talk, then just play a game, read a book, or watch a favorite TV program with them. Children often feel that if bad things happen to them it must mean they are bad. As a friend or family member, you can help preserve their feelings of self-worth by spending time with them, hugging them and praising them for their accomplishments.

Continuing normal patterns as much as possible will help give a child a feeling of security. One friend whose father was killed on the mission field when she was seven remembers the birthday party her mother prepared for her just two days after her father's death as one of the nicest parties she ever had. I'm sure that party was difficult for her mother, but it helped the little girl feel there were still some traditions and some people she could depend on. As a teenager, she also remembers feeling sad as she watched other girls being kissed by their dads, but she is grateful for her two brothers who gave her lots of special attention and many hugs.

A boy whose father has died needs the attention of a man, someone who will take him to a ballgame or sit in the stands and cheer for him while he plays on the school team, confirming that he is a person of value.

The program at a recent Compassionate Friends convention included a special panel for bereaved siblings. The most common complaint from the young people was how fearful and over-protective their parents had become since their brother or sister's death. The parents' fear is understandable, but it is important to give the remaining children freedom to live normal lives. At least be open with them. "Since your brother died in a car accident, I'm nervous about letting you take the car. I'll do a lot better if you make every effort to be home on time and always call if you are delayed."

This past summer a ten-year-old girl stayed with us for two weeks. One evening she went bike riding with some friends. While they were gone, we heard several sirens in our area. I got so nervous, I was almost in tears by the time the girls returned. I told her that those sirens reminded me of the sirens I heard the night Nate died, and silly as my reaction may seem, I would really feel better if she went riding when Glen or I could go with her. Once she understood my feelings, she accepted my request quite willingly.

Getting over your fears and giving children room to enjoy life will take a while, but if you're honest with each other, your children will be more likely to cooperate with you.

Teenagers may have a particularly difficult time dealing with the death of someone close. Because of their youth, their grief is often minimized by adults, yet teenagers are old enough to feel the pain very deeply and also to feel the pain of others. While grieving for Nathan, I discovered that when I shared my feelings with some of his teenage friends, they were able to empathize with me better than many adults. The young people at Nate's school weren't afraid to acknowledge their grief. They were the ones who thought of giving me the roses at graduation and presenting the slide show at baccalaureate. They dared to speak openly about their love for Nathan and how much they missed him. I often received notes like these:

I just wanted to take this time to tell you that I'm still thinking of you and praying for you. I hope my smile and questions of how you're doing make your days easier. Let me know if you need someone to talk to or to do something for you.

Mickey

When I see you in the halls, I can see that you are having a very hard time. I want you to know that if there was anything in the whole world that I could do that would lessen your hurt, I would gladly do it. When I see you hurt, it just hurts me so much inside I can hardly stand it. I can now truly under-stand 1 Corinthians 12:26 [NIV] that talks about the body of Christ: "If one part suffers, every part suffers with it; if one part is hon-ored, every part rejoices with it." We all hurt with you, Mrs. Heavilin!

Natalie

On the first anniversary of Nate's death, I received this note from one of my former students:

I just wanted you to know that I was thinking about you today. I know this must be a difficult time for you. Nathan was *very special* to all of us, and even though I miss him greatly, I'm sure I can't begin to understand the depths of your love for him and the mixed emotions you must have at this time. I only pray that God will continue to comfort you with the awesome fact that Nathan beat the rest of us home!

Andy

We need to be careful not to rebuff young people's attempts to express their sorrow. Sometimes we can help them by verbalizing feelings they might be having. "When an older brother dies, sometimes a younger brother can feel very lonely. He might even be mad at his brother because he left so suddenly. Do you ever feel like that?"

If our children don't seem comfortable sharing their feelings with us, we need to help them find someone they can talk to — school counselor, teacher, pastor, youth worker, grief counselor, or peer.

Reach out to bereaved children, spend time with them and find out how they're feeling. They are innocent, fragile rosebuds who need gentle, loving care. Be a rose and help them through this difficult, confusing time.

The Rose
of
Tenderness

O Lord, don't hold back your tender mercies from me!
My only hope is in your love and faithfulness. Otherwise
I perish, for problems far too big for me to solve are piled
higher than my head (Psalm 40:11,12, TLB).

After Nate's death, many people said, "You'll find this crisis will draw you closer together." Now, after several years of working through our differences, I believe we are closer, but that wasn't true at first. For many couples crisis pulls their families apart because crisis will accentuate nearly every aspect of your marriage, weak or strong.

A salesman named Joe was trying to sell us a motorhome, and in a talkative and friendly manner he asked about our family. We explained that we had two married children and then told him about Nate.

He started asking some very knowledgeable questions. "How have you dealt with the grief? Your marriage seems to be OK. How have you managed that?"

I said, "Joe, what's your story? I sense you have dealt with a major loss."

His eyes filled with tears as he recalled,

> My second wife and I had been married just a few months. My son came to visit one weekend. He was riding his bike near our house when he was struck and killed by a drunk driver.
>
> He was my only son. When he died, everything in my life changed. For the next year I spent all of my time following the manslaughter trial. Nothing else mattered. The driver was given a light sentence which didn't satisfy me, and I was consumed with anger.
>
> My new wife didn't know my son well, and she couldn't relate to my grief. Soon, we stopped talking to each other. I stayed away from home as much as I could. I blamed myself — why did I let him ride on that busy street? I should have gone with him.
>
> I became more and more depressed. Our marriage ended within a year.

Joe looked wistfully at Glen and me and said, "If you can survive the death of three sons, you've got something pretty special!"

Joe was right. Any couple whose marriage weathers a crisis as severe as the death of a child is in the minority today.

Compassionate Friends states between 75 and 85 percent of the couples who lose a child will divorce within the first five years after the death.

Will you be one of the statistics? You don't have to be if you're willing to work at keeping your marriage together. Let's look at some factors which tend to break up a marriage.

GUILT. It is natural for a person to experience guilt, deserved or undeserved, when a loved one dies, but it is destructive when the guilt is allowed to fester and grow out of proportion. We need to talk to someone openly about our feelings.

When Nate died, one of my first thoughts was, *Why didn't I go to the game with him? This wouldn't have happened if I had been there.*

By the time I told Glen how I felt, I had built a strong case against myself. In an effort to help me analyze my feelings, Glen said, "Why didn't you go to the game?"

"Well, I had been to one on Tuesday and I was going to the game on Friday. Also, I would have had to drive to Hemet alone, fifty miles away, at night, and I've never done that before."

Glen very logically said, "So even if you had gone, you probably would not have been in the same car with Nate."

"Well, probably not," I admitted.

Glen continued, "If you had been in the car with Nate, how could you have prevented the crash?"

"I don't know, but mothers are supposed to be able to protect their children!" I sobbed.

In a very loving and yet logical way, Glen helped me see how unwarranted my guilt was.

BLAME. Although it may not be justified, couples often build a case of blame against each other. A husband may think, *If she hadn't let him play in the front yard, he wouldn't have been able to run out into the street,* even though they had both allowed the child to play in the front yard on previous occasions. Whether or not the husband is justified in blaming his wife, these feelings must be carefully and sensitively exposed, discussed, and eliminated, or a wedge will start to form between them.

LACK OF COMMUNICATION. Often a wife will tell me, "He never talks anymore. I don't know what he's thinking. He eats and sleeps at our house, but that's it. We're strangers." A spouse's grief may be so all-consuming that he can't risk talking about it for fear of losing control. Getting this person to open up will take a lot of tender, patient probing.

NOT UNDERSTANDING SEXUAL NEEDS. When Laura and Jim's daughter died, they were both overwhelmed with grief, but they responded differently. Within a few days after their daughter's death, Jim wanted to have sexual relations with Laura; he needed that emotional release and the assurance that she still cared for him. Laura was indignant. "How can you think about enjoying yourself like that when we just buried our daughter?"

Couples who have lost little children may have opposing responses also. I heard one young father say, "I think we should have another baby right away." His wife responded, "I'm afraid of getting pregnant. I don't ever want to love anyone that much again."

These are all normal responses but they can cause difficulty if they are not discussed and resolved. A wife who is afraid of being sexually intimate will still usually enjoy being held and tenderly cared for. Be sensitive to each other's needs, concerns and fears. Give each other time to work through his or her feelings.

EXPECTING TOO MUCH OF OURSELVES. I am quite melancholic in my temperament and am very much the martyr, so it takes me a long time to admit I have had enough. One evening in May, after Nate had died in February, I reached a point of total desperation. I sobbed, "I can't ever go back to school. I have to get out of here."

Glen could have just given me a pep talk saying something like, "You're a big girl now. You need to get ahold of yourself and get on with life."

Instead he chose to show me the tenderness I needed, and very calmly said, "Where do you want to go?"

I really didn't care, but the first place that popped into my mind was Hawaii. That was a Thursday evening; we left on Sunday! I'm sure the travel agent wondered about us. She asked, "Which islands do you wish to visit?"

Glen and I shrugged our shoulders and he said, "We don't care. You decide."

Then she queried, "What hotel would you like to stay at?"

Again the answer came, "We don't care. You decide."

We really didn't care. We knew we had to get away, but the place or the hotel simply didn't matter. Nothing mattered right then except that our son was dead and we were hurting.

With mixed emotions, I said goodbye to my remaining two children on Mother's Day morning — I felt a twinge of guilt because I was leaving them, but I knew we had to do this. Was I running away? Perhaps — but I decided it was all right. Even Jesus had to get away from the crowds once in a while.

I wrote in my journal:

Today is the day we fly to Hawaii! I still can hardly believe it, but I am getting excited. That excitement is mixed with twinges of remorse and guilt. Remorse because of why we need this trip, and guilt because we're trying to enjoy ourselves so soon after Nate's death and because I've never been away from my kids on Mother's Day. I felt funny leaving them.

Today I have been able to handle the verse about "forgetting the things that are behind." I believe I am beginning to desire that, but until now, that verse just made me angry. I have been fighting against that verse, so I know this desire to "forge ahead" has to be from the Lord. It surely didn't come from me. Perhaps a new day is dawning — one in which we can build a future with new memories and let the old memories rest. I hope so.

The next day:

I awoke this morning with the same old thought, *Nate is gone.* But it didn't hit me like a kick in the stomach; it was more like a "nagging backache." It's always there, but I'm learning to live with it.

The trip to Hawaii was good for us; it was our first extended vacation without the children in twenty-four years. The trip helped us begin to build some memories which didn't include Nate and it gave us a temporary release from the pressures at home. Since that time, Glen and I have traveled to Japan and made a return trip to Hawaii. Those trips took effort on our part. Most of the time it would have been easier to stay home and wallow in our misery. I didn't enjoy tending to all of the details traveling requires, and it was hard to move out into a new environment, but it did help. Now we don't wait for the pressure to build up so high. We take small trips often, and our marriage has become stronger because we have spent time alone with each other away from all of the reminders and problems.

LACK OF SPECIAL ATTENTION. In the face of the personal and family tragedy that we were dealing with, I needed a way to communicate to Glen that he was important to me. Nathan was important and his death was important, but Glen needed to feel that in spite of all that was happening around him, he was important, too.

After some of the dust had settled, I said, "Glen, I want you to choose a day and take off work. In fact it would be even better if you took a day and a half."

"Why?"

"I'll tell you later."

When the day came, I gave Glen a list of instructions. "Get in the car. Drive down Cajon Avenue. Turn left at the next traffic signal. . ." We followed this little sequence of clues and ended up at a Victorian mansion which was a bed-and-breakfast inn. In the trunk of our car nestled a wicker picnic basket with a chilled bottle of sparkling cider, cookies, cheese, fresh fruit, and a tape recorder with a cassette tape of "Music for Lovers." We spent the evening in this Victorian mansion with a player grand piano, and I had the opportunity to show Glen some tenderness and say, "In spite of all we're going through, you're important to me. You are a very important person."

PERSONAL RESPONSES TO GRIEF. Glen and I recently led a workshop on "How We All Grieve Differently" for the National Convention of The Compassionate

Friends in Omaha, Nebraska. When we finished, Nancy, one of the conferees, stood and gave a beautiful example of how she found a way to meet her husband's needs even though they were grieving differently and he seemed unable to express his feelings to her.

Before our son was killed my husband and I always had a good marriage. Even though we've had lots of tragedy, we always managed to get through everything. But after our son died, my husband just clammed up. He didn't want to have anything to do with me; he didn't talk. He just went to work, went to the cemetery, came home, and that was it. This went on for two years.

I felt completely abandoned. I had six other kids and they looked to me for emotional help, but when it came to me, I was on my own. This was the worst time to be on my own. I didn't understand him. I began to resent the fact that my husband wasn't there for me as he had always been when we went through so many other things.

Finally, I don't know why I thought of it, but I got a notebook and I started to write to him in the notebook. I left it in his underwear drawer where he would have to see it. I wrote about all sorts of things, things I was feeling, things I knew he was feeling. I wrote about how good he was all through our marriage when different things happened and told him what a great guy he was. I told him I didn't know what had happened, but I felt I didn't have him anymore.

He always read my notes, but he never said a word. After a whole year of me writing in the notebook and sticking it in his drawer, he finally came out of his shell. It was almost

three years after our son's death, and now
our marriage is better than it has ever been.
Having a good relationship with him again
is worth all of the effort I put forth.

Even though they were grieving differently, and her
husband had isolated himself, Nancy found a way to
extend loving tenderness to him.

In an article on coping with heartbreak, Robert Veninga states:

When a husband and wife share a heartbreak,
each must plot his or her own defense. You
cannot plan the defense strategies of your
partner nor can you plot a joint defense, for
a heartbreak really is a solitary experience.[1]

In many ways grief is a solitary experience, but you
can be a rose of tenderness as you make the effort to
tell your spouse how you feel and what your needs
are. We are extremely fragile people at this point, but
we will become stronger as we can spread the fragrance
of our roses around us and we realize what is important
to us. Don't let go of those loved ones you have. Don't
let the differences part you. Bring yourselves together.
Keep looking for the roses. They're there.

The Rose
of
Uniqueness

I will praise thee; for I am fearfully and wonderfully made:
marvellous are thy works; and that my soul knoweth right
well (Psalm 139:14).

When I first met Glen Heavilin, I knew I had met my perfect match. He was quiet, steady, and dependable. He thought through everything he did, and didn't speak until he had something important to say. He was all of the things I wasn't!

He listened quietly while I talked on and on and was content to let me get involved in lots of committees and social groups while he stayed home and studied or watched the children. His mood was predictable — peaceful and happy — while mine constantly changed.

He provided me with dependability and I provided
him with variety.

It really has been a good match. We've had very
few major arguments. I have disagreed with him often,
but I soon discovered it was no fun to argue with someone who wouldn't argue back. So we began to do it
Glen's way — we reasoned with each other and settled
things peacefully. His way worked just fine until
Nathan's death.

We were grieving differently and our marriage was
being tested. It hadn't been that way with the deaths
of Jimmy and Ethan, and we knew we now had to
find out what the problems were. Before, our strength
had been in our love, our concern, and our admiration
for each other. After Nate's death those things didn't
seem to be enough. We were disagreeing on everything
and we couldn't understand why.

With the other boys' deaths, there was no one to
blame, no legal hassles. With Nate's death, waiting for
all the legal and insurance matters to be settled was
like waiting for the benediction at the funeral, and it
slowed down the healing process. Going to court again
and again, only to find the trial date has been postponed each time can be wearing on anyone. A bereaved
person is already so vulnerable; each postponement
can be like a hammer blow driving him lower and
lower into the depths of despair.

Our case was postponed eleven times and then
actually was settled on the one day we didn't go
because the district attorney felt the trial would just
be postponed again. We felt cheated. We did not have
a chance to hear the man declared guilty; nor did we
have a chance to speak regarding his sentencing — one
more frustration in the long line of bewildering legal
proceedings.

An organization such as MADD, Mothers Against
Drunk Driving, could have given us professional help,

but there was no chapter in our area, and we were too tired and confused to try to get help beyond our local area. I wish a counselor or a friend had been able to do that for us.

Having to deal with the manslaughter case was very discouraging because we felt so uninformed and excluded. No one ever volunteered any information; we had to dig to find out what was going on. When the case was finally resolved, the man was sentenced to three years probation and not a day in jail.

If you are a pastor or counselor, or a friend of the bereaved person, please understand that that person needs to express his feelings in whatever way is comfortable for him without fear of condemnation. I was angry at a justice system that in my opinion didn't hand out a punishment equal to the crime, and I became quite cynical. Some of my feelings were not the best, yet I needed to express them. But when people responded with, "You're a Christian; you shouldn't feel like that," I was devastated.

I thought, *It's true that I'm a Christian, but I'm still having these feelings. Is there something wrong with me?* It was much more helpful when someone let me say how I felt and then worked with me to resolve those feelings without condemning me.

In regard to the insurance we felt vulnerable because we had so little control. Our objective was to get the insurance settled as soon as possible. The amount of the settlement concerned us to a point — we felt it had to be adequate because to us it represented Nate's "worth" and we could not accept the possibility we might receive less because he was "not an only child" or because he was "only seventeen." On the other hand, it didn't have to be exorbitant; we had few bills to pay and Nate wasn't here to spend it on.

The other families felt they needed to take plenty of time to make sure the doctors had discovered all of

the injuries their children had incurred — the larger
the settlement, the more they would have available to
"protect their child's future." This was hard for us since
Glen and I had discovered years ago that only God
can protect our children's future.

We realized their goals were different from ours, but
Glen's reaction to that was opposite to mine. He felt
we had no choice but to wait since our insurance company did not want to settle with us until they could
settle with everyone. He even suggested we should
wait patiently!

Well, I waited because I had no choice, but I certainly
didn't wait patiently. I fussed and fumed. I wanted
Glen to call the other families and *demand* that they
understand what they were doing to us by dragging
everything out so long. Glen wouldn't do that, and
he wouldn't let me do much either, so I spent my time
being mad at Glen. Our marriage was full of stress.
Many times it took several vigorous walks around the
block together before we could even speak to each other.

We were both vulnerable and our weaknesses began
to reveal themselves. My need to talk began to bother
Glen. He didn't want to hear all about my difficult
days because his days were difficult, too. My up-and-
down moods turned into all down ones, and I cried
frequently.

The insurance situation and the manslaughter trial
together wore me down, and I didn't want to reason — I
wanted to fight. Glen didn't look like a peacemaker to
me anymore; he looked like Mr. Milquetoast. I wanted
him to protect me from the cold, cruel world and make
people be nice to me. Instead, he kept telling me I
should be patient with the insurance company and
with the court system. The more I nagged him to get
involved, the more uninvolved he became.

That fall I attended a seminar led by Florence Littauer
where she talked about temperaments and gave each

person a temperament test. After I discovered what my temperament was, I went home and had Glen take the same test. Then I began to understand why we were having difficulty. Our temperaments were opposite which is typical of most couples. Most of the time that's wonderful because your partner has strengths where you have weaknesses and you can build each other up.

If you're a serious person, it's nice to have someone who is fun, can tell jokes, and sees the funny side of life. But those same things that are fun and make you mesh together when everything is going right also tend to pull you apart when you're going through tragedy.

I believe that as married couples we often don't understand each other and so we do not recognize our partner's needs. Those needs are built into their temperaments.

There are four basic temperaments, Sanguine, Choleric, Melancholy, and Phlegmatic. Glen's major temperament is Phlegmatic: "low-key personality, easy going and relaxed, calm, cool, and collected, happily reconciled to life, an all-purpose person."[1] Some of the Phlegmatic's weaknesses are: "avoids responsibility, quiet will of iron, too compromising, resents being pushed, stays uninvolved, resists change."[2]

My temperament is a split of Choleric and Melancholy: "must correct wrongs, strong-willed and decisive, moves quickly to action, insists on production, idealistic, persistent and thorough, sees the problems."[3] Some of a Choleric/Melancholy's weaknesses are: "impatient, demanding of others, remembers the negatives, moody and depressed, self-centered, persecution complex, depressed over imperfections, hard to please, critical of others, dislikes those in opposition, unforgiving."[4]

No wonder we were having trouble! Our basic responses to adversity were so different. As I listened to Florence I began to realize that Glen was not responding differently from me just to buck me, and he wasn't necessarily saying I was wrong. We simply were looking at the world through different eyes.

Each temperament is driven by different goals. The Sanguine wants to have fun; the Choleric wants to have control; the Melancholy wants to have it right; and the Phlegmatic wants to have peace. So Glen's goal was to have peace, "Don't rock the boat"; my goal was to have control and have everything right. When Nathan died, all of our goals were challenged.

Glen recalls:

> Marilyn mentioned the manslaughter trial which is a criminal operation run by the district attorney's office. In some countries of the world the victim has a voice in criminal cases, but the victim has no voice in our criminal justice system. Marilyn is Choleric/ Melancholy. The Melancholy wants everything to be perfect and the Choleric wants to control things to make them just and fair and equitable.
>
> Now how do you control the criminal justice system? The Phlegmatic says, "Anybody in their right mind knows you cannot control the criminal justice system."
>
> Marilyn would say, "Why don't you call the district attorney and find out what's happening with the case?"
>
> My brain says, "Why would I want to do that? We'll find out what's happening with the case when the district attorney does something with it." I learned how to call the district attorney. Marilyn learned how to, as gently

as possible, prod me into calling the DA. She
really did. You have to *gently* prod a Phlegmatic. If you sternly prod a Phlegmatic, he
sets his heels in and says, "I will not do it,"
and I've done that many times.

It is important to take the time to recognize that
others are different, and to give them the space to be
different. Be creative and look for ways you can meet
the other person's needs. It will pay off.

While I am talking basically about the husband and
wife relationship, you can adopt these principles with
your children and your friends as well. Our daughter
Mellyn has a temperament much like her father's. She
did not want me to cry; she wanted things to stay as
normal as possible. She didn't need a lot of people
around and often retreated to her apartment when our
house became crowded with people. I needed lots of
people around and became depressed when everyone
left.

Since Mellyn didn't want me to cry, I made sure I
didn't cry in front of her. One day when Mellyn was
in our home, I was very depressed. Because I felt I
couldn't cry in front of her, I went into my bedroom,
called my friend Nancy, and told her I needed help.
Nancy quickly came to the house and told Mellyn I
had called her. When Mellyn came to the bedroom
and found me sobbing, she was very hurt because I
hadn't told her I was having a hard time.

We finally realized neither one of us was wrong but
we were grieving differently, and we needed to make
room for each other. I began to understand that Mellyn
missed Nate terribly even though she didn't show it
in the same ways I did. Mellyn learned that each time
I cried, I healed just a little bit more.

Our son Nathan was a strong Phlegmatic just like
his father. I had learned to adjust to Glen, but when

one of my children was so different from me, I had difficulty. As a Choleric mother I insisted each child make his or her bed every day, but Nate couldn't see any need in making his bed because after all, "I'll just get back into it tonight." I'm the type who wants to have everything done two weeks ahead of time, but Nate would say, "Why hurry to read the book? I have two days before I have to turn my book report in."

I wish now I had understood the temperaments when I was rearing my children. I've had to go to my remaining children and say, "I need to apologize to you for some of the ways I worked with you because I just didn't understand."

Understanding our temperaments has helped us to realize what our normal, first reaction would be in a given situation. Now we are able to work on our deficiencies and emphasize our strengths without feeling the other person is disapproving of our behavior.

A while back my daughter called and said, "Mom, Mike and I took the test and he is Melancholy/Choleric and I am Melancholy/Phlegmatic. Mrs. Littauer says that people usually marry opposites, but we're almost the same temperament."

I laughed and said, "Honey, that's just fine — unless you have a Sanguine child."

There was a gasp and, "Oh, Mama!"

Rearing a bubbly Sanguine who never looks at a schedule can drive the methodical Melancholy to distraction unless he understands the temperament traits and realizes the child is not being different just to be disobedient or to upset the parents.

The Sanguine's basic underlying drive is to have FUN. If he loses his fun, he gets depressed. The Sanguine child can't sit very long in class, and he will have difficulty listening to a lecture unless the speaker is entertaining. Sanguines want to get involved, and when they enter a crowd, they see an audience to entertain. They have a child-like style of emotion even when they reach adulthood. Their emotions can be very short-lived and changeable. They cry hard but a few minutes later they can go on to something else.

Sanguines will come bouncing into a room and never know a stranger. They make wonderful waitresses, receptionists, salespeople, comedians, and talk show hosts. They talk very easily to everyone. If others don't talk, they just keep on talking and don't even notice because they like to hear themselves talk. When they're angry, their anger generally doesn't last long. Once they have said everything they want to say, it's over and everything is fine. They can't understand what's wrong with all of those other people who are mad at them. When a Sanguine is grieving, he will try to forget his troubles by having fun.

Sanguines need constant encouragement and approval. You can keep a Sanguine going as long as you keep telling him he's doing a good job and keep recognizing his efforts.

The Cholerics' major drive is for CONTROL. When Cholerics go through trauma, they try to deny the pain by becoming totally absorbed in their work, a hobby, or a social cause. They'll work furiously and may not want to come home for fear it will be too emotional and they might lose control.

The one emotion Cholerics may display is anger, and their anger is generally rooted in impatience because things aren't moving, people are slow, and they don't see any progress. They also may display anger when they're actually feeling sadness.[5] It is almost impossible for Cholerics to say "I'm sorry," even if they feel it inside because admitting blame makes them feel they're losing control or becoming vulnerable to other people.

Cholerics have a need for appreciation of responsible and dutiful endeavors. They need acknowledgment of their hard work. Some men come home after putting in many extra hours at work to hear their wives say, "I don't feel you love me anymore. I never see you. You don't seem concerned. You aren't involved with us."

The husband responds, "But I work sixty hours a week for you. What more do you want?" From the Choleric's point of view, he is showing love by the amount of work he produces, but it may not mean a thing to the wife who is home alone and needs to have some attention from her husband. It helps if we can understand how each temperament directs our method of demonstrating love and concern for others.

Melancholies want PERFECTION. They want to be able to depend on how things are going to be; they're generally quite methodical. They will have medium highs but they have very low lows. A Melancholy trying to deal with grief may go into a deep depression.

When Melancholies are depressed, everybody knows it. Some of them get to the point where they don't talk at all. I didn't get that low, but I did have occasions when I felt a cloud of doom was over my head and I couldn't get away from it. At those times, having people around me who wanted to have fun was totally obnoxious to me. I couldn't understand the responses of those people because I felt deeply about everything.

In *Personality Patterns,* Lana Bateman refers to the Melancholies as "green stamp collectors." When you hurt them they take a green stamp and paste it into their book. If somebody else hurts them, they paste down another green stamp. They may be holding their feelings inside but they have all of these green stamps in the book. When that last green stamp gets in the book, it may be something very simple, it may not be nearly as big a hurt as something on the first page of their green-stamp book, but they may explode.[6]

One day after we moved into our new home, we couldn't find something (I can't even remember what it was), but after I looked and looked and couldn't find it, I just fell apart. I sobbed and sobbed. It had very little to do with what I couldn't find, but my emotions had built up through our move and the dam finally broke. Poor Glen was standing there trying to think what he had done wrong.

The Melancholy's underlying need is "Creative Tenderness."[7] Taking Glen to the Victorian mansion was creative tenderness. Melancholies are very good about thinking of ways to show creative tenderness but they tend to marry a temperament that doesn't really notice all of their effort. The Melancholy thinks up wonderful ideas and wishes someone would do those things for him. I've had to learn to communicate my needs and desires to others.

Phlegmatics have a great desire for PEACE, sometimes peace at any price. They fear conflict, and it is very hard for them to express their emotions. Phlegmatics may show little emotion even when they are experiencing grief, and those around them may think they have already worked through their grief. In truth, it could be they have not handled it at all. It may take them several years before they deal with their loss. They often respond to anger with sadness which is just the opposite of the Choleric who usually responds to sadness with anger. When these two temperaments marry each other, and that will frequently happen because opposites tend to marry, they are likely to have problems.

As a Choleric, when I'm sad about something, my sadness may come out in anger as it did when I was faced with the insurance problems. I wanted Glen to go tell the other families what this was doing to us. Why couldn't they understand? I was angry because I was hurt. Glen pulled back and wanted to be really quiet about it. He wanted to keep peace.

I said to Glen, "You aren't protecting me. You aren't taking care of me and meeting my needs. What's wrong with you? I don't know you anymore." And I'm sure Glen felt the same about me.

Phlegmatics need a sense of value — they need to feel they're important. Because they have difficulty showing emotion or expressing their thoughts, they are often lost in the crowd and it's easy for people to assume they have no thoughts. The partner who sticks with them, though, will eventually find out what's going on in the Phlegmatic's mind.

Understanding the temperaments will help when you and your family are in a crisis. The death of a child may be the worst thing you have ever faced in your life, and differences in temperaments can increase the stress within the entire family. You need to remember that other family members loved that child as much as you did. Don't alienate them. Reach out to them. Pull them in so you can enjoy together the love and memories you shared and try to learn the underlying needs of each other. Recovering from grief can be a life-changing experience. (One book I recommend to help you better understand the different temperaments is *Personality Plus* by Florence Littauer.)

It is important that we give other family members room to grieve in their own way, but we also need to work at keeping in touch with each other. Some of the things Glen and I did were to talk and listen to each other. I brought the temperament test home and I said, "I know you don't like this kind of thing, but I need you to listen." As I read the characteristics of the Phlegmatic, I described Glen right down the line.

Glen said, "Let me see that."

Sure enough, this test had him pegged. I asked, "What do you want me to do for you? How can I help you?" Then he did the same with me and I said, "I need to talk. I need to tell someone how I feel, why I get mad, upset and frustrated every time this trial gets postponed. Yet I realize that when I talk to you it upsets you, and you feel helpless. I know you can't do anything about the justice system, but I still need to get it out."

Finally Glen said, "Well, when you get upset, why don't you call Joan or go see Nancy?" This was a concession for Glen because we always had the policy that we didn't talk about our personal problems outside of our family. He realized, though, that in this situation he was helpless. He couldn't do anything about it, and when he heard me complain he just got more depressed and felt more inadequate. He said, "You need to have someone you can talk to who won't feel the load like I feel it."

Once I aired my feelings with someone else, I could come home and love Glen.

We began to understand it was all right to be different. Just because I was doing something one way didn't mean the way Glen was doing it was wrong.

Then we listed our needs and desires. Glen said, "I need to know that you aren't disappointed in me, that you aren't angry with me or blaming me because this insurance situation isn't going better." I hadn't realized that when I let off steam about our situation I was just pushing Glen deeper into a hole of guilt. I just knew I needed confirmation that he thought I was doing all right and that he still liked me.

We planned special times to be together. We drove to the mountains, walked around Lake Arrowhead, and talked. Sometimes we just drove to a nearby regional park, ate dinner in our motorhome, and talked. Where we were didn't matter, but talking did. We became re-acquainted and slowly began to discover those special traits that had drawn us together originally.

I can now say after twenty-eight years of marriage that we really are enjoying those differences again. Glen's sense of humor, for a while an irritant to me, is now wonderful — nice and dry. I appreciate his ability to be a peacemaker although right after Nate's death I didn't want peace. Glen does not enjoy traveling and speaking frequently, but he has given me room to do so because I love it. He is my support system, and even travels with me as much as he can. We back each other up now, but it has been a struggle to learn that we can. It took time to understand each other.

How thrilling to realize our precious Lord created each of us to grow in His garden as unique, priceless roses.

Each of us can be a rose to the people in our families who are grieving in a way different from the way we are. Reach out to them and say, "It's OK that we're different, but the most important thing is that we stick together. We need each other. We loved this person together. We need to share our hurt together." You can be a rose of uniqueness if you make room for those you love.

The Rose
of
Love

But God showed his great love for us by sending Christ to die for us while we were still sinners (Romans 5:8, TLB).

Without the Rose of Love there would be no book because I would have no hope. The Rose of Love is my best Friend, my Comforter, and my Redeemer. He is revealed in the Bible as God, Jesus Christ, and the Holy Spirit.

If you have not met Jesus Christ before, please let me tell you about Him. Jesus became my Redeemer when I realized, at a very early age, that in my own power I would not be able to go to heaven when I died. I recognized I could not remove the sin which was in my life and I needed help. My mother explained

that Jesus Christ loved me and He had died for me
as a sacrifice for my sins even before I was born. At
that moment I invited Jesus Christ into my life and
He became my Savior.

Through the years, as I have learned more about
God and as He has let me see how much He loves
me and cares for me, He has become my best Friend.
He never criticizes me; He always listens when I need
to talk; and He is constantly looking out for my best
interests.

The Bible refers to Him as the God of all comfort:

> Blessed be God, even the Father of our Lord
> Jesus Christ, the Father of mercies, and the
> God of all comfort; who comforteth us in all
> our tribulation, that we may be able to comfort
> them which are in any trouble, by the comfort
> wherewith we ourselves are comforted of God
> (2 Corinthians 1:3,4).

As I have experienced the deaths of three of my
sons, God has become my Comforter. He is always
available to me; He is not impatient with me; He
doesn't judge me or rebuke me for admitting I hurt.
God has experienced sorrow. He, in fact, was a bereaved
parent, because He, too, had a Son who suffered and
died. But the exciting news is God's Son didn't stay
dead. He conquered death for each of us so that we
can have the hope of spending eternity with Him in
heaven. We also can have the hope of seeing our loved
ones again.

I have vivid memories of a special night when Nate
was five years old. I was tucking him into bed and
he seemed restless and unable to settle down. I asked
him if there was a problem. He squirmed a little and
then said, "I'm not sure I've invited Jesus into my
heart."

I asked him why he wanted to invite Jesus into his life. "Because I've done some wrong things, and I want to make sure I'll go to heaven."

I listened as Nathan prayed and asked Jesus to come into his heart and live with him. After that there was no doubt in Nate's mind. He referred to the event often. As he grew, we saw the effect of the decision in his desire to study God's Word and in his submissive attitude toward us and toward God.

How thankful I am I can look back on that evening and have confidence I will see Nate again.

And now, dear brothers, I want you to know what happens to a Christian when he dies so that when it happens, you will not be full of sorrow, as those are who have no hope. For since we believe that Jesus died and then came back to life again, we can also believe that when Jesus returns, God will bring back with him all the Christians who have died (1 Thessalonians 4:13,14, TLB).

Jesus understands my sorrow. He experienced abuse, rejection, and death. He wept when others were grieving. He felt their sorrow and He feels my sorrow and yours. Jesus comforts us so we can comfort others. He wants us to pass it on.

When Jesus left this earth, He promised that the Holy Spirit would come to dwell in all Christians: "And I will pray the Father, and he shall give you another Comforter, that he may abide with you for ever" (John 14:16).

When I first became a Christian, I did not understand the ministry of the Holy Spirit in my life. However, in my late twenties I met a group of people who talked about the Holy Spirit as though He were a real person! Through that Bible study I discovered that the Holy

Spirit dwells in me and His purpose in my life is to convict and convince of sin, but He is also with me to comfort me. He sees my needs even before I do and He asks God the Father to meet my needs.

Those days when I was so discouraged and couldn't even reach out for help, the Holy Spirit would know my needs and would plant the thought in a friend's mind, "Call Marilyn; she needs you today."

The Holy Spirit is the one who convicts me when I harbor unforgiving attitudes toward others. He also gave Glen and me the desire and ability to rebuild our marriage relationship.

God, in the person of the Holy Spirit, comforts my heart, assures me I will see my children again, and gives me the power to live my life as a victor rather than a victim.

It is my prayer that this little book will be helpful to all who read it whether they know Jesus as their personal savior or not. However, it is important for you to understand the reason I have been able to accept Jimmy's, Ethan's and Nathan's deaths. It is primarily because of the source of strength available to me through Jesus Christ, the Rose of Love.

If you do not know Jesus, I encourage you to invite Him into your life now. Jesus has extended the invitation to you:

> Come unto me, all ye that labour and are heavy laden, and I will give you rest (Matthew 11:28).

Some of you may not want to deal with this right now. Perhaps you have "put God on hold." You may be asking a lot of questions: How could a God of love let my child suffer and die? or Why my child? I talked with one bereaved parent who recalled, "At first I asked why, and then the question came back, Why not? Who am I to say my family should be exempt from trouble? Am I really more deserving of a trouble-free life than my neighbor or my friend?"

I cannot solve all of life's complex problems, and I, like you, certainly have asked why and haven't come up with profound answers. But I do know God loved each of us enough to offer His only Son as the perfect and permanent sacrifice so that you and I might have eternal life.

The same God who loved Glen and me enough to provide a sacrifice for our sins also allowed some people we loved dearly to die sooner than we thought they should. I can't explain God or God's ways, but I am confident enough of His love for me, and for Jimmy, Ethan and Nathan, to say, "I trust Him and you can trust Him, too."

If you are experiencing grief, I'm sure you have many questions. You probably feel heavy laden, and you undoubtedly wish you could cast your burdens on someone else so that you could rest. I urge you right now to talk with Jesus and tell Him this is the heaviest burden you have ever had to bear. You are grieving because of a great loss and you are so very tired. Hand Him your burden and ask Him to carry it for you.

Jesus is the most beautiful rose of all. Take a deep breath of the fragrance of His love and compassion and then perhaps you can share His fragrance by reaching out to others who are hurting, too.

Let the Rose of Love stand in the center of your bouquet of December roses.

The Rose
of
Victory

But despite all this, overwhelming victory is ours through Christ who loved us enough to die for us (Romans 8:37, TLB).

W hen the police came to tell my friend Patsy her daughter Suzie had been in an accident, Patsy sensed it was very serious. Yet as she drove to the hospital, she reasoned, "Everything seems normal. Traffic is moving properly; people are walking down the street; the moon is shining; and the stars are still in the sky. If Suzie were dead, the whole world would stop. Everything would be in chaos — life could not proceed in its normal pattern."

However, when she arrived at the hospital, she discovered Suzie had died, and Patsy's world turned

upside down even though the rest of the world did
not stop.

I felt the same way after Nate died. I would watch
people complacently shopping or enjoying a meal in
a restaurant, and I wanted to shout, "How can you
do that? Don't you know Nate is dead?"

When you're facing a severe crisis, your world does
stop. Nothing matters. Life loses its edge. The big
question is, Does the world ever start turning again?
You may wonder, *Will little things ever matter? Will I
ever get excited about anything? Will I ever enjoy life
to its fullest again?*

After Jimmy and Ethan died, we did eventually begin
to enjoy life again. I got excited about Christmas for
my children, and I did learn to enjoy long-awaited
events. But once in a while I still cast a nostalgic look
at what might have been.

Whenever I see twins, I wonder what it would have
been like to raise Nathan and Ethan together. When
I see a large family, I wish I could have raised all five
of my children instead of just three. This year Jimmy
would have been twenty-two, and his birthday was
difficult for me. As I looked at other boys his age, I
felt cheated because I didn't get to watch him grow up.

My heart winces when I hear a mother yell angrily
at her children or threaten to "give them away" if they
don't behave. I'm tempted to reprove her and say,
"You should appreciate your children and thank God
you have them."

Our whole family really enjoyed Mellyn's wedding,
but even Mellyn remembered the two brothers who
were absent. The pillow which held the wedding rings
was a satin one used to hold flowers at Ethan's funeral,
and the flower girl carried a white wicker basket from
Jimmy's funeral. Mellyn explained, "I want all of my
brothers to be represented."

We did quite well at Matt's wedding a year and a half after Nate's death until we posed for a family picture. Then we didn't dare look at each other because we all knew what the others were thinking: *When we had the family picture taken at Mellyn's wedding, Nate was with us. He should be here now.*

As I watched many of Nate's classmates participate in Matt and Debbie's wedding, I wondered if Nate could see. Did he know his big brother married one of his best friends? Oh, how I wished I could talk with him!

Recently, I watched Nate's friend Christian perform with his college glee club. I was thrilled for him, but my eyes filled with tears as I remembered when he and Nate had talked of attending college together.

Afterward, I told his mother how much I enjoyed the concert. Her response helped me a great deal. "I'm sure you enjoyed the program, but I know you must have been thinking what it would have been like to have Nate there because I was thinking about him, too." It feels so good to know others have not forgotten him.

Life is never the same after a loved one dies or you suffer some other major loss. But life can be good again — different, but good. As I look back over the past few years, I can mark turning points in my healing process: The first trip to Hawaii allowed me to step outside of my situation, removed me from some of the pressures, and gave Glen and me time to talk. Moving from full-time to part-time status at the school gave me freedom to spend more time at home and visit with friends when I felt the need to talk.

Another turning point came almost two years after Nate's death. I drove to the cemetery, sat on the grass near Nate's grave, spent some time thinking over the happenings since the accident, and then realized I was getting better. As I walked away, I knew I would not be coming again soon. For me, it was time to move ahead.

Making the decision to speak publicly about my experiences gave me a new purpose and a sense of new beginning, but it was not easy. Shortly after the funeral I received a card from a representative of MADD. I quickly put the card away and said, "I'll never get involved with any crusades."

Later, Florence Littauer invited me to speak at the HOPE Conference (Helping Other People Emotionally) in Anaheim, California. I worked hard, prepared my notes, and practiced my speech, but the evening prior to the conference I sat in Nate's room and sobbed for hours. I was certain I would break down in the middle of my talk.

Many of my friends attended HOPE, and I asked them to sit in the back of the auditorium so that I wouldn't be affected by their tears. They prayed fervently, and God gave me the strength to present my story without losing control. I was amazed at the response of the people; they said I had really helped them!

Shortly after that I was invited to attend the training for the MADD Speakers Bureau. I made it clear I was attending simply to gather information; however, to finish the course we were required to present a talk on drunk driving and send a tape of the speech to our trainer. I spoke to the student body at Nate's high school and was thrilled at the students' response. One of the girls in the audience asked me to speak to her youth group, and then someone else invited me to speak at a Kiwanis meeting. During the next six months I spoke forty-five times to all types of groups from Al-A-Non to Kiwanis, to all of the driver's education classes in the San Bernardino City high schools.

As I walked into Juvenile Hall recently and they locked the doors behind me, I thought, *Why am I doing this? Do I really think I can tell these boys anything they don't already know? Will it make a difference? Perhaps I'm wasting my time.* As the boys walked in, I felt a love for them immediately. They listened intently and afterward crowded around me to look at some pictures of Nate.

A few weeks later I received a large manila envelope containing thank you notes from each of the boys. As I read them, tears filled my eyes. One note said,

> From now on when I go to a party I'm going to try not to drink and drive. I would also like to say you really fascinate me by the way you make your life happy from helping others who may have lost a loved one, instead of dwelling on the loss of your own children.

Another boy wrote:

> You did teach me how the victims feel. I have driven drunk before, and I'm going to be your rose in December because I'm never going to do it again and I'm going to spread the word. You taught me the unbelievable pain victims go through in losing an innocent loved one in this situation. Thank you.

Do notes like this make it worth losing Nate? NO, but they help to make his life and his death count. When I think of the other families who have lost a loved one and felt pain similar to mine, nearly 26,000 each year since Nate's death, I realize if I can persuade even one person not to drink and drive, if, because Nate died, I can save even one family from this pain, or if I can help grieving parents pull their lives back together because Jimmy, Ethan and Nathan died, I am establishing a living memorial to my boys. That's a rose!

When my friend Diana's ten-year-old son Jimmy died in a shooting accident, Diana was devastated. She had lived in Phoenix only a few months and felt completely alone in her grief. After seeing a program about Compassionate Friends on television, she called the headquarters to find out how to get in touch with a group in her area. She was disappointed to hear there was no chapter in Phoenix, but the national director gave her the name of another bereaved parent who had been trying to start a chapter and suggested Diana help her. Diana thought, "How can I do that? I can't help anybody else; I'm the one who needs help." But Diana did eventually become involved and was a founding member of the Phoenix chapter.

When she moved to Riverside, California, four years after Jimmy's death, Diana started a new chapter of Compassionate Friends. In the past five years she has offered a listening ear and given hope to hundreds of bereaved families throughout Southern California. Through her support of other grieving parents, Diana has given purpose and meaning to Jimmy's life and to his death.

Jan and her husband each had a painful childhood. When they married they felt their love would overcome the past. Then he went to Vietnam. When he came home, he was even more troubled, and a few years later their marriage fell apart, leaving Jan to raise her two children alone. In 1984 her former husband was in a car accident and his brain was severely damaged. Since that time Jan has become involved in trying to get recognition and help for Vietnam veterans. She goes to the hospital where her ex-husband is a patient, and often has spent time counseling families of other brain-damaged victims. She is also a leader of a program for single parents in her church. Jan has accepted the responsibility to turn her experiences into help for others.

Jasmine was born with Down's syndrome, but her parents praised the Lord because tests showed she did not have any heart defects. However, when little Jasmine was five and a half months old the entire family contracted the flu. Jasmine became very ill and it was soon discovered that she did in fact have two holes in her heart. She died two weeks later of heart failure.

Her mother Colleen recalls, "At first I didn't see how I could help anybody else; I was just trying to help myself." Colleen met with a professional counselor regularly for several months and kept good notes on the counseling techniques which helped her the most. After she went back to her position as a childbirth educator, co-workers would call her when a client's child died, saying, "Since you've gone through this, I think you'll know just what to say." Now Colleen frequently counsels with bereaved parents of young infants. She states, "I'd rather have Jasmine back, but there are great rewards in sharing the pain of these parents. It's a memorial to Jasmine's life."

During the Vietnam War, a bullet injured Cornelius's spinal cord. He is confined to a wheelchair, but that hasn't stopped him from developing excellent counseling skills and working with high school students. When Cornelius says, "I care about you," students forget about his wheelchair and begin to open up to a concerned and caring friend. Cornelius made a choice not to let his physical disability limit him in any other way.

A newly bereaved parent said to me, "It bothers me to think I might become a better person, that I might benefit from my daughter's death. It doesn't seem anything good should come from a child dying."

I responded, "You have three choices. You could try to stay the same and not have her death affect you; you could give up on life and become a societal dropout; or you can become a stronger, more sensitive, wiser person because your child lived and died."

If you have lost someone you love, you will have to make a choice, too, but don't feel you must rush into any big decisions. Do your grief work. Give yourself time. Seek God's heart, and let Him guide you into the unique purpose He has for you.

It may be months or even years before you realize you are actually enjoying the "ordinary" things of life again. I always enjoyed cooking and entertaining, but after Nate's death, cooking took too much energy and entertaining seemed purposeless.

Before he died, when the children were home mealtime was always an event. We looked forward to being together and catching up on the news of the day. After Nate's death, Glen and I had difficulty eating at the dining room table when it was only the two of us. Nate's absence was just too obvious. We moved to another room to eat when we were alone. After three years, we moved into a different home, and then we finally were able to establish a pattern of eating in the dining room again.

There will come a day when I can enjoy watching a high school basketball game, and some day I will look forward to Christmas again.

Eventually, when someone asks the simple question, "How many children do you have?" I will be able to say "two" without feeling my stomach churn.

God will lead us to victory, and He does *make* all things work together for good. I am beginning to see glimpses of that "good."

A few months ago I attended the funeral of another young man who was killed by a drunk driver. I didn't want to go, but I felt I must offer my comfort to his wife and young child. While I was at their home, I met a woman whose children I had known, but I had not met Sandy before. I talked with her and openly shared our loss of Nate and how we were trusting God to get us through this experience.

After the funeral, Sandy came up to me and said, "I need to talk with you."

I said, "Fine, what about?"

Sandy responded, "I'm ready to take a step with God, and I think you can help me!"

That evening, over pie at a local restaurant, I was able to lead my new friend Sandy into a personal relationship with Christ.

Through her tears, she commented, "Nate may be gone, but his life lives on."

I know her statement is true. The evidences of Nathan's impact on the world are all around me. I see his influence on our friends, on his teenage friends, and on our family. I know Glen and I are stronger people because of what we have faced in the years since Nate's death.

If my boys have the opportunity to look in on me from heaven, I hope they can say, "We may be gone, but our mom is living on. She hasn't given up. She is still serving God, and she is a stronger person who is walking closer to God because she had three sons who lived and died and are now living with God."

Friend, don't give up. As you go through this December of your life, God is willing to walk beside you. He understands when you have hard days; He understands you are grieving because of the terrible loss you've suffered.

Look around you and see the roses: the friend who is standing with you, the memories of your loved one, the Scripture God has given you, the kindnesses others have offered, the work God is doing in your heart.

Gather those roses, and let their refreshing aroma fill your life with a confidence that Jesus hears and cares about you. Reach out to the Lord, and put your hand in His so He can lead you to VICTORY.

Keep looking for the roses!

Notes

CHAPTER TWO

1. This quote is generally credited to Sir James Barrie, the author of Peter Pan.

CHAPTER FOUR

1. S. I. McMillen, M.D., *None Of These Diseases* (Westwood, New Jersey: Fleming H. Revell Company, 1963), pp. 73-74.
2. Lewis B. Smedes, "Forgiveness: Healing the Hurts We Don't Deserve," *Family Life Today* (January 1985), pp. 24-28.
3. Joni Eareckson Tada and Steve Estes, *A Step Further* (Grand Rapids, Michigan: Zondervan Publishing House, 1978), pp. 15-16.

CHAPTER FIVE

1. Joseph Bayly, *The Last Thing We Talk About* (Elgin, Illinois: David C. Cook Publishing Co., 1973), p. 66.

CHAPTER EIGHT

1. Janice C. Harris, ACSW-CSW, and Angela Bennett, "Helping Children Cope With Death in the Family" (Hurst, Texas: Mothers Against Drunk Drivers, 1984, pamphlet).

CHAPTER NINE

1. Robert L. Veninga, "How To Cope With Heartache," *Ladies Home Journal* (November 1985), pp. 74-82.

CHAPTER TEN

1. Florence Littauer, *Personality Plus* (Old Tappan, New Jersey: Fleming H. Revell, 1983), pp. 18-20.
2. Ibid.
3. Ibid.
4. Ibid.
5. Lana Bateman, *Personality Patterns* (Dallas, Texas: Philippian Ministries, 1985), pp. 3-12.
6. Ibid.
7. Ibid.